THE BATTLE OF THE ATLANTIC

ROY CONYERS NESBIT

SUTTON PUBLISHING

First published in 2002 by
Sutton Publishing Limited · Phoenix Mill
Thrupp · Stroud · Gloucestershire · GL5 2BU

British Library Cataloguing in Publication Data
A catalogue record for this book is available from the British Library

ISBN 0-7509-2912-X

Typeset in 10/14pt Sabon.
Typesetting and origination by
Sutton Publishing Limited.
Printed and bound in England by
J.H. Haynes & Co. Ltd, Sparkford.

CONTENTS

ACKNOWLEDGEMENTS

I am extremely grateful to the large number of friends and colleagues who have helped with the content of the chapters in this book. They are:

Joe Autey; Soloman Belinky USAAF; David Benfield; Fred Biggs RAFVR; Sqn Ldr John A. Botham RAF (Ret'd); Flt Lt Norman D. Boynton RAFVR; Flt Lt Ralph Barker RAF (Ret'd); Hugh J. Budgen; Ms Anne Carroll WAAF; Warr Off Bill Carroll RAFVR; the late Air Marshal Sir Edward Chilton KBE, CB, RAF; Sqn Ldr Ian Coleman RAF; Sqn Ldr Dudley Cowderoy RAFVR; Ms E. Lettice Curtis ATA; Gordon C. Dalton RAAF; Barry Davidson (Civil Aviation Authority); Chris Davies; Peter Elliott (RAF Museum); John Evans (Peterchurch Publications); Flt Lt Graham Fairhurst RAF (Ret'd); Maurice Fellows; the late Gp Capt Geoffrey Francis DSO, DFC, RAF; Frederick M. Galea (National War Museum of Malta); Wg Cdr John C. Graham DFC*, RAF (Ret'd); Flt Lt Victor H. Gregory DFC, RAFVR; Brian Hansley; Flt Lt Eric N. Harrison RAFVR (No. 228 Sqn Assn); Gp Capt Charles W. Hayes OBE, RAF (Ret'd); Roger Hayward; Henry Holloway in South Africa; the late Mrs Molly Jones (sister of Amy Johnson); the late Flt Lt Ronald Martin RAFVR; John A. Miller; the Revd Fred E. Moore DFC, RAFVR; MEng Phil Nobbs RAF; Michael Oakey (*Aeroplane*); Bob O'Hanlon RAFVR; the late Philip N. Owen RAFVR; Ken Perfect; the late Flt Lt A.M. 'Tony' Puckle MBE, RAFVR; Clive Richards (Air Historical Branch of the MoD); the late Gp Capt F.C. 'Dickie' Richardson CBE, FRIN, RAF; Richard Riding (formerly of *Aeroplane Monthly*); Peter Rivers; Alan G. Ross; Mrs Sandra Sanders; Flt Lt Ernest Schofield DFC, RAFVR; Mrs Beryl Seal-Morgan WAAF; the late Fg Off Fred H. Shaw RAFVR; the late Ms Constance Babington Smith MBE, WAAF; Tom G. Smith (Rolls-Royce Heritage Trust); Ken Snelling DFC, RAFVR; Halvor Sperbund in Norway; E. Richard Staszak; R. Steiner (de Havilland Heritage Centre); Mrs Adèle Stephenson (airline pilot); Mrs Bente Mary Svasand in Norway; Deryck Thurman RAFVR; Dana Timmer (Howland Landing Ltd); Richard T. Tosaw; Ms Diana Barnato Walker MBE, ATA; Fg Off Bryan Wells RAFVR (RAF Amateur Radio Assn); Cpl Tim Wilson RAF; James A. Woodward RAFVR; Martin Woodward.

Lastly, I should like to thank the two aviation artists who have contributed paintings to this book. They are Martin Postlethwaite GAvA and Charles J. Thompson GAvA, ASAA, GMA, EAA.

CHAPTER ONE

RE-LEARNING
THE LESSONS

It was Winston Churchill who coined the phrase 'Battle of the Atlantic' to describe a long-fought and bitter struggle, of which he later said: 'The only thing that ever frightened me during the war was the U-boat peril.'

The command of the seas was essential to Britain's survival. One of the tasks of the Royal Navy was to ensure that the country's merchant fleet could sail with safety over the world's seas and oceans. The majority of Britain's raw materials, all her petrol and much of her food came from abroad. Without these supplies, her armed forces could not operate and the country would be starved into submission. It would have no option but to surrender to a vicious tyranny, with disastrous consequences for the whole free world. The North Atlantic was a part of the ocean where the enemy could obtain a decisive victory, and the German strategists were well aware of this. Indeed, they were at one stage quite confident of ultimate success.

Certainly the U-boat arm of the Kriegsmarine, under Admiral Karl Dönitz, came closer to destroying Britain's capacity to wage war than did the Luftwaffe under Generalfeldmarschall Hermann Goering. Dönitz was a master strategist and tactician, devoted to his task and possessed of a U-boat arm equipped with the best of German technology and manned by crews with an almost suicidal devotion to duty; in contrast, the flamboyant and bombastic Goering made mistake after mistake and failed to develop his force to meet the demands of war, in spite of the bravery of the aircrews under his command.

The Battle of the Atlantic was fought in appalling conditions of hardship. Both sides were implacably intent on destroying their opponents. Long periods of gruelling work and acute discomfort were punctuated with sudden and violent actions that often resulted in death, either quick or protracted. Not only did the seamen have to fight their enemy but also the forces of nature at their most turbulent – mountainous seas, great storms and numbing cold. The fight took place in the air as well as at sea, and indeed it was the growth and increasingly effective use of air power which eventually tipped the scales in favour of the Allies. As so often in the war, British technology came to the aid of its hard-pressed fighting men. Coupled with the industrial might of the USA, this technology finally brought victory.

When war was declared on 3 September 1939, the Royal Navy was considered the most powerful in the world, but its duties were world-wide. The Home Fleet, including the Channel Force, the Humber Force, the Nore Command and the Western Approaches Command, consisted of 7 battleships, 2 battle cruisers, 4 aircraft carriers, 22 cruisers, 82 destroyers, 21 submarines, 38 minesweepers, 8 anti-submarine trawlers and 14 escort vessels. Other great forces served in the Mediterranean Fleet, the China Station and the East Indies Station. There were also the North Atlantic Command, the South Atlantic Command, and the America and West Indies Station. Within the latter three, the warships covering the Atlantic consisted of 14 cruisers, 13 destroyers, a seaplane carrier, 6 escort vessels, 4 submarines and 2 minesweepers. This force was supported by the Royal Canadian Navy with 6 destroyers. There was also a large Naval Building Programme in Britain which included 5 battleships, 6 aircraft carriers, 19 cruisers, 52 destroyers, 11 submarines, 4 escort vessels, 4 minelayers and 40 minesweepers.

On 21 July 1937 control of the Fleet Air Arm had at last been passed back from the RAF to the Admiralty, although over two years were to elapse before all the arrangements were completed. On the outbreak of war this air arm consisted of 16 first-line squadrons and 11 catapult flights, backed up with 11 second-line squadrons. Pilots in the first-line squadrons flew Fairey Swordfish, Fairey Fulmars, Supermarine Walruses, Blackburn Skuas, Blackburn Rocs, Fairey Seafoxes and Sea Gladiators with the Home Fleet, the Channel Force or the America and West Indies Station. Some of these aircraft were obsolescent, but the torpedo-carrying Swordfish biplane was more effective than its 'string bag' appearance suggested.

The RAF's Coastal Command was the most neglected of its three home-based commands, priority in the belated rebuilding programme having been given firstly to the offensive power of Bomber Command and secondly to the defensive capabilities of Fighter Command. The sixteen squadrons of Coastal Command were equipped with about 195 front-line aircraft at the outbreak of war. Of these, 135 were Avro Ansons, a reliable monoplane suitable for short-range reconnaissance but with inadequate armament and bomb-carrying capacity. There were 9 Lockheed Hudsons, an American aircraft chosen to replace the Ansons. The older section of the flying boat force consisted of 15 obsolete Saro Londons or Supermarine Stranraers, but there were also 12 new and splendid Short Sunderlands, with more under construction. The torpedo-carrying strike force consisted merely of 22 obsolescent Vickers Vildebeest biplanes, but more effective Bristol Beauforts were being built to replace them.

In spite of the inadequacies of its equipment, Coastal Command was considered an elite force by those who flew in it, with the flying boat squadrons rated as the most prestigious. Special qualities were required by men who flew for long hours over the oceans, out of sight of land, before the days of automatic pilots and radar. Only the steadiest and most accomplished pilots were selected for this work. Moreover, the navigators needed to be skilled in 'dead-reckoning' calculations as well as the esoteric art of astro-navigation, since wireless bearings in those days had a very limited range and in any event radio silence was required in wartime. These skills had been developed by mariners over the centuries and adapted for use in the air, initially by the Royal Naval Air Service in the First World War. Coastal Command maintained a strong affinity with the Royal Navy and officially came under the control of the Admiralty for its wartime operations, although in practice this meant working in close cooperation. The men who served in it at the outbreak of war formed the nucleus of a Command which, in time, was to have one of the most destructive effects on the U-boat arm.

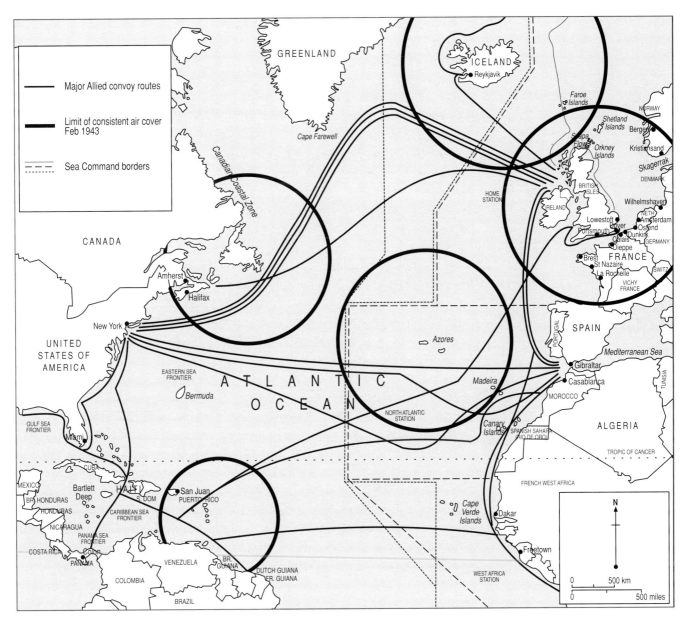

The Battle of the Atlantic.

The Royal Navy also worked in partnership with the French Navy. This too had its world-wide commitments, but its main strength was concentrated in the Mediterranean. However, it contributed its 'Force du Raid' in the North Atlantic, consisting of 2 modern battle cruisers, an aircraft carrier, 3 cruisers and 10 destroyers.

Although there were inadequacies with their escort vessels and air arms, the Allied warships available in September 1939 seemed overwhelmingly superior to those of their enemy. The German Navy, or Kriegsmarine, was disposed in two main areas, facing the North Sea and the Baltic Sea, with the warships able to move easily to and from each area. There were 2 fast battleships, 2 ancient battleships, 3 so-called 'pocket battleships', 5 cruisers, 17 destroyers, 13 torpedo-boats (the size of small destroyers), 10 motor torpedo-boats, 8 minelayers, 6 submarine flotillas with 45 operational U-boats, plus a U-boat School with 12 non-operational U-boats.

The Kriegsmarine had no aircraft carriers, although the *Graf Zeppelin* was being built. As with the Royal Navy and the French Navy, the larger warships carried Arado Ar196 floatplanes for reconnaissance purposes, either catapulted from the deck or hoisted into the sea. The service could count on some support from the shore-based Luftwaffe, but the latter was not organised according to function as in the RAF. Instead, it consisted almost entirely of four large air fleets, or Luftflotten, each supporting the armies in its area, as one might expect with the greatest continental power in Europe primarily intent on territorial expansion. Luftflotte 1 operated in north-eastern Germany, Luftflotte 2 in north-western Germany, Luftflotte 3 in south-western Germany and Luftflotte 4 in south-eastern Germany. Apart from these Luftflotten, however, several smaller units were specifically assigned for operations with the Kriegsmarine, including those reconnaissance floatplanes carried on the larger warships. There were 31 Heinkel He59s, 81 He60s and 8 He115s, all employed on reconnaissance or air–sea rescue and mostly fitted as floatplanes. There were 63 Dornier Do18 flying boats and 21 Heinkel He111 bombers. Lastly, 12 Junkers Ju87s and 24 Messerschmitt Bf109s were designated for service with the aircraft carrier *Graf Zeppelin*, although this was never completed.

By the late 1930s the British Empire and Commonwealth had developed the greatest maritime trading organisation in the world, with over 7,500 merchant vessels plying their trade and using port facilities throughout the world. Of these, about 3,000 deep-sea merchant ships and tankers, plus 1,000 coasters, were registered in Britain, constituting a total of 21,000,000 tons. On the outbreak of war the Ministry of Supply requisitioned every merchant ship available, from tiny cargo vessels to the great passenger liners for which the country was famous. All these remained the property of their original owners, who effectively became agents of the government, responsible for maintaining their ships but subject to official directions as to the content of their cargoes and numbers of passengers, together with the times they could sail and the journeys they could make. The owners were covered by government insurance, provided they conformed with their orders. All new ships built in Britain, purchased from America or captured from the enemy were subject to the same regulations.

The convoy system was immediately introduced, and indeed one such convoy set out from Gibraltar to Cape Town the day before war was declared. The benefits of this system had been apparent from the days of Horatio Nelson, although its use had been intermittent. In the First World War, when at one stage Britain had been brought almost to her knees by sinkings from U-boats, the re-introduction of escorted convoys had reduced losses to less than a tenth of their previous number. At the beginning of the Second World War the convoys outward bound from Britain were prefixed OA if they left from the Thames or OB if they left from Liverpool. Homeward-bound convoys from Freetown in Sierra Leone were designated SL, while slow convoys from Halifax in Nova Scotia were lettered HX and fast convoys HXF.

The commanders of these convoys were known as Commodores and all were volunteers from the Royal Naval Reserve. Many were over the normal age of wartime service and some were in their late sixties, but all were men of great experience and distinction. They did not command the ships they sailed in but flew a white flag with a blue cross to demonstrate their status. Royal Navy ships flew the White Ensign, its auxiliary vessels the Blue Ensign, and merchant ships the Red Ensign. The masters of the merchant ships were a gritty and independent breed who seldom took kindly to naval discipline. They often became impatient with the delays caused by forming convoys of up to a hundred ships outside a port and were resentful of the dangers of collision at night in rough seas. Some of

This rare photograph of the docks at Hamburg was taken by the Luftwaffe in February 1938. Many vessels have been identified by experts in Germany. The battleship *Bismarck* is under construction in the Blohm & Voss shipyard, to the right of the six corrugated roofs at the bottom of the photograph. To the right of this shipyard is the armed yacht *Grille*, of 2,560 tons displacement, which was employed as a minelayer in the early months of the war and sometimes as a state yacht. The cruise liner *Wilhelm Gustoff*, used as a hospital ship during the war, is immediately above the six roofs. On the left of her in the photograph is the heavy cruiser *Admiral Hipper*, of 13,900 tons displacement.

Author's collection

them contrived ways of sailing independently, until the perils of doing so became startlingly apparent.

The men who served in this Merchant Navy were similarly tough. Anticipating the need a year before the war, the British government called for volunteers to swell their ranks and about 13,000 men had responded by September 1939; they were of all ages and ranged from experienced navigation officers to young deck-boys. These formed a reserve pool which could be called upon to serve in any type of ship. The men were later joined by many European nationals who had escaped from occupied countries, as well as Lascars from India and other volunteers from Arab and African countries. In 1942, the strength of the Merchant Navy rose to about 120,000 men. Apart from the dangers of death or injury from enemy action, these men experienced the hazards of handling heavy equipment in rolling seas, together with the possibility of hypothermia on deck or heat exhaustion in engine rooms. It is small wonder that the behaviour of some of these men was less than angelic in their periods ashore, in spite of the numerous welfare organisations that were formed for their benefit. The words of the eighteenth-century writer and lexicographer Samuel Johnson were still valid: 'Being in a ship is being in a jail, with the chance of being drowned.'

The convoy system also had its serious shortcomings, for in 1939 there were insufficient Royal Navy escorts, and only a few of these had the endurance to accompany the slow convoys all the way across the North Atlantic. Most of the available escorts were engaged with the troopships and merchant vessels carrying the British Expeditionary Force and its equipment across the Channel to France, in addition to protecting the considerable volume of coastal traffic along the east coast of Britain from attack by German warships and aircraft. The remaining destroyer escorts accompanied the Atlantic convoys only as far as 12°30' West, some 100 miles west of Ireland, where they met and escorted a homeward-bound convoy which had left Halifax protected by an armed merchant cruiser. The outward-bound convoy then continued for two more days before the vessels dispersed to sail independently to their various destinations.

Nor was Coastal Command capable of providing an effective escort for these convoys. The Ansons had a radius of action of about 250 miles but the need to circle a slow-moving convoy for much of the time and then to conserve fuel for emergencies meant that their 'time on station' was very limited. Of course the Sunderland I, with a radius of action of about 900 miles, was far more effective, but there were too few of these flying boats. There was no airborne radar so that sightings, such as the ominous feathered wake of a periscope, were purely visual. Moreover, if they were able to attack, their bomb-loads were almost useless. Airborne depth-charges had not yet been produced and instead they carried anti-submarine bombs which had been developed between the wars. The 100lb version had little destructive power and in any event the U-boats had usually disappeared below the surface by the time these were dropped. Machine-gun bullets of 0.303-inch calibre could be used against enemy gunners but did not penetrate the hulls of U-boats.

One such attack occurred on 5 September, two days after war was declared, when an Anson of 233 Squadron from Leuchars in Fife was on patrol over the west coast of Scotland. The crew spotted a submarine on the surface and the pilot dived to release his bomb-load, two anti-submarine bombs of 100lb each. These exploded on impact with the sea and pieces of metal pierced the Anson's fuel tanks. Shortly before the Anson reached base the fuel ran out but the pilot made a good ditching in St Andrew's Bay. The crew got into their dinghy and were picked up unharmed. Meanwhile, the submarine had received no more than a severe shaking and was able to reach port. Embarrassingly for the RAF, it was HMS *Seahorse* of the Royal Navy.

On another occasion, eleven days later, two Blackburn Skuas from the aircraft carrier *Ark Royal* bombed the Type VII *U-30*, commanded by Oberleutnant Fritz-Julius Lemp, as it was submerging. Once again the anti-submarine bombs exploded on impact with the water, bringing down both aircraft. Lemp surfaced and rescued two survivors, who were taken into captivity. In spite of such mishaps, there is no doubt that the presence of aircraft had a strong deterrent effect on the commanders of U-boats, who crash-dived immediately they were sighted and thereafter were reluctant to press home attacks.

One of the first Sunderland Is was serial L5802, delivered to 210 Squadron on 24 October 1938. It was later transferred to 204 Squadron and then to 201 Squadron. It is shown here at Pembroke Dock with the code letters SE of 95 Squadron, which flew out to Freetown in Sierra Leone during February 1941 to cover the waters of the South Atlantic. L5802 was finally written off after an accident on the night of 15/16 January 1943, when on the strength of No. 4 Operational Training Unit at Alness on the Cromarty Firth.

Imperial War Museum TR108

The Avro Anson was the most ubiquitous aircraft in Coastal Command on the outbreak of the Second World War, after entering service for reconnaissance and escort duties in March 1936. Powered by two Armstrong Siddeley Cheetah IX engines of 350hp, it had a range of only 700 miles and could carry only 480lb of bombs. It was armed with a fixed machine-gun firing forwards and another in the turret. Although inadequate by later standards, the Anson was highly regarded for its reliability, being known as 'faithful Annie'. This example was on the strength of 502 Squadron at Aldergrove in Northern Ireland.

Author's collection

It was believed by the British at the outset that the main threat to the convoys came from enemy surface raiders. These could be pocket battleships, cruisers or armed merchant ships, although their range was limited unless rebunkering facilities could be provided, usually from supply ships in designated positions. Much of the activity of the Ansons and Hudsons in the early months of the war was devoted to patrolling the North Sea in search of such warships, while the Royal Navy hunted the oceans to intercept those known from intelligence sources to be at large.

On the other hand, it was also believed that the menace of the U-boat had been removed, partly by the invention in 1918 of an underwater detecting device, named 'Asdic' after the Allied Submarine Detection Investigation Committee which had been responsible for its development, and partly by the depth-charges carried by escort vessels. Asdic was a transmitter/receiver, fitted in a metal case under the hull of a vessel, which sent out sound waves and created an audible echo in the form of a high-pitched 'ping'. The instrument could be turned through a full circle, thus providing the direction of the U-boat. This had been a considerable advance in technology, but it suffered from several disadvantages: it was difficult to distinguish the 'ping' of a U-boat from those of rocks or shoals of fish; the depth of the object could not be ascertained; and the ship had to moderate its speed to avoid the 'pings' being drowned by the noise of water rushing past the instrument. Thus by the time the ship arrived over a possible position in order to drop depth-charges over its stern, the target might have disappeared. Asdic also became less effective when new tactics were employed by the wily Karl Dönitz, as will be described later.

One of the most surprising post-war disclosures is how few U-boats were available in September 1939 for the Atlantic theatre. Of the 57 on the strength of the Kriegsmarine, 45 were operational. Of these, 23 were coastal types suitable only for the North Sea or the Baltic Sea, while the remaining 22 were ocean-going types. When war was declared, only 7 of the latter were on patrol in the Atlantic, although others were dispatched to join them. Nevertheless, this small number had an immediate and alarming effect on the British.

In the evening of the first day of war the liner SS *Athenia* of 13,851 tons was sunk by the Type VII *U-30* when about 250 miles north-west of Ireland, en route from Liverpool to Montreal. The commander of the U-boat, Oberleutnant Fritz-Julius Lemp, asserted that he was under the impression that the liner was a British armed merchant cruiser. There were over 1,100 passengers on board, of whom 112 were killed, including 28 Americans. This action contravened Hitler's orders to avoid offending neutrals, and the Germans did their best to expunge the sinking from their records. However, any compunction about the feelings of neutrals did not last long. From 23 September the Kriegsmarine was allowed to sink any merchant ship using wireless. Restrictions were relaxed further on 17 October when it was permitted to sink any ship identified as hostile, with the exception of liners. In the following month it was decreed that any Allied merchant ship could be sunk without warning. The era of unrestricted warfare at sea had begun.

On 17 September the Royal Navy suffered a bitter blow when the aircraft carrier HMS *Courageous* of 22,500 tons displacement was torpedoed about 225 miles south-west of Ireland by the Type VII *U-29*, commanded by Kapitän-leutnant Otto Schuhart. Unknown to the British, the German intelligence service B-Dienst was able to decrypt the Admiralty cipher and was aware that the aircraft carrier was cruising in this area, escorted by only two destroyers. She was hit by three torpedoes and went down in 15 minutes, taking with her 518 men and two Swordfish squadrons, nos 811 and 812. The remaining carriers of the Home Fleet were withdrawn from the wasteful work of hunting U-boats, which was the naval equivalent of searching for a needle in a haystack.

Another humiliating disaster for the Royal Navy took place on the night of 13/14 October when the Type VIIB *U-47*, commanded by Kapitänleutnant Günther Prien, penetrated the approaches to Scapa Flow and then passed through the fixed defences, which were still incomplete, to torpedo the old battleship HMS *Royal Oak* of 29,150 tons displacement. She capsized 13 minutes later, with the loss of 833 men including the commander of the Second Battle Squadron, Rear-Admiral H.E.C. Blagrove.

Meanwhile, in August 1939 the pocket battleships *Admiral Graf Spee* and *Deutschland* had left their home ports. The former reached the great expanses of the South Atlantic and the Indian Ocean, where British merchant ships were still sailing independently and without escort. She sank nine ships totalling 50,000

A Blackburn Skua taking off from the deck of the
aircraft carrier HMS *Courageous* in February 1939. This
carrier, of 22,500 tons displacement, was torpedoed
south-west of Eire on 17 September 1939 by the Type
VIIA *U-29*. She sank in less than 15 minutes, with the
loss of 518 men.

Courtesy of Aeroplane

tons before being intercepted and damaged in December by a cruiser force of the
Royal Navy off the River Plate. Her captain ordered his crew to scuttle her on
13 December. The hunt for this warship had tied up no fewer than 15 British and
French cruisers, 3 aircraft carriers and 3 battle cruisers, but at least the successful
action gave the British public something to celebrate. The *Deutschland* swept the
North Atlantic for Allied ships but the convoy system had cleared the normal
shipping routes. She found and sank only two ships sailing independently, before
returning to Germany.

The 'phoney war' which characterised the military situation on the Western
Front in the early months of the war did not apply to the Royal Navy, the Fleet
Air Arm or the RAF's Coastal Command. There was activity along the east coast
of Britain, where magnetic mines dropped by the Luftwaffe and attacks by
aircraft on shipping took a steady toll. In more distant waters the U-boats sank
sixty-eight Allied merchant ships in the first two months, totalling 288,686 tons,
most of them sailing independently. Nine U-boats were sunk before the end of
the year, three by mines and six by the Royal Navy. Not a single U-boat was sunk
by aircraft, although Coastal Command attacked on forty occasions and caused
some damage to eight U-boats.

U-boats also had their own problems in this period, for the depth-keeping
mechanism in their torpedoes proved unreliable and the firing pistols sometimes
failed to function when they struck enemy vessels. Moreover, Dönitz controlled
too few ocean-going U-boats to begin the 'wolf-pack' attacks on convoys which

The *Deutschland* class pocket battleship *Admiral Graf Spee*, of 12,100 tons displacement, was armed with six 28-cm and eight 15-cm guns, and was capable of 26 knots. She made a foray into the South Atlantic in the early weeks of the war but was damaged off the River Plate on 13 December 1939 by gunfire from the cruisers HMS *Exeter*, HMS *Ajax* and HMS *Achilles*.

Author's collection

caused so much havoc at a later stage of the Battle of the Atlantic. During the first four months of the war his force succeeded in sinking only four merchant vessels sailing in convoy; all the other ships sunk had been sailing independently.

Something of a lull occurred during the bitter winter of early 1940 (when, incidentally, the author was under training as a very young but eager volunteer in the wartime RAF). Sinkings of Allied merchant vessels and U-boats continued at a reduced scale. The first occasion when an aircraft could share credit in one of the latter took place on 30 January 1940 when the Type VII *U-55*, commanded by Kapitänleutnant Werner Heidel, was hunted by Sunderland serial N9025 of 228 Squadron, flown from Pembroke Dock by Flying Officer Edward J. Brooks. The U-boat had attacked and sunk two ships in a convoy passing round the north-west tip of France but had been damaged by depth-charges and was unable to dive. The Sunderland bombed and strafed the boat, which was scuttled when the convoy's escorts closed in. Eleven survivors were rescued.

There was public exhilaration in Britain when the fleet auxiliary *Altmark*, returning to Germany with 299 prisoners taken by the *Admiral Graf Spee*, was spotted off Norway on 16 February by a Hudson of 220 Squadron from Thornaby in Yorkshire. Warships of the Royal Navy were directed to intercept the enemy vessel in Norwegian waters, where they rescued all the prisoners.

The first 'kill' of a U-boat from the air was made, almost accidentally, by Bomber Command. On 11 March 1940 Blenheim IV serial P4852 of 82 Squadron, flown by Squadron Leader Miles V. Delap from Watton in Norfolk, was hunting surface craft off Borkum when it came across the Type VII *U-31*, commanded by Kapitänleutnant Johannes Habekost, which was engaged on sea trials after a refit. Delap dived and released four 250lb general-purpose bombs in a salvo. These were far more effective than the 100lb anti-submarine bombs and sent the U-boat to the bottom with all hands.

In early 1940 many of the ocean-going U-boats were withdrawn for Hitler's forthcoming invasion of Denmark and Norway, intended partly to protect his essential supply of high-grade iron ore supplied by Sweden for the German war machine. The Führer feared that the British intended to land an expeditionary force in Norway and also wished to protect his northern flank for the great attack by the Wehrmacht on the Western Front. This fear had been reinforced by the *Altmark* incident in February.

At this time, British Signals Intelligence (Sigint) was providing little information and most intelligence came from neutral countries via diplomatic channels. It was known that Germany had stopped Army leave and was paying attention to the Danish frontier. RAF reconnaissance photographs indicated a concentration of shipping at Kiel, but generally preparations by the British to counter an invasion were too late. It was not until the afternoon of 7 April that a Bomber Command aircraft reported a German battle fleet moving towards Norway. By then the Royal Navy was laying mines in Norwegian waters but the Home Fleet was sailing on a course too far to the north and was unable to make an interception. The assault began on 9 April, an undeclared state of war which was codenamed Operation Weserübung. The Wehrmacht rolled into Denmark and brushed aside the small resistance which could be offered. Fliegerkorps X, formed for this purpose, dispatched 500 air transports with paratroops and other airborne soldiers to Norway, supported by about 100 fighters and 320 bombers. Almost the whole of the Kriegsmarine took part, carrying units of an Army corps to land simultaneously at Narvik, Trondheim, Bergen, Christiansand and Oslo. Over the next few days the Home Fleet engaged units of the Kriegsmarine, losing

The first U-boat to be sunk in the war was the Type IXA *U-39*, commanded by Kapitänleutnant Gerhard Glattes, west of the Hebrides on 14 September 1939. It attempted to sink the aircraft carrier HMS *Ark Royal*, but the torpedoes exploded before reaching the target. The escorting destroyers HMS *Faulknor*, HMS *Foxhound* and HMS *Firedrake* then dropped depth-charges which blew *U-39* to the surface before it finally foundered. The whalers in this photograph were picking up survivors, forty-four of whom were rescued.

Author's collection

4 destroyers, a sloop and a minesweeper. But the Royal Navy sank 2 German cruisers, 9 destroyers, a minelayer and 4 U-boats.

The Norwegians had not mobilised and were unprepared, but fought bravely to the best of their ability. Their air force and navy were almost wiped out, but shore batteries accounted for one German cruiser and severely damaged another, as well as a torpedo-boat. It was not until 14 April that British contingents landed at Namsos and near Narvik in support of their ground forces, followed by others at Andalsnes. Initial cover was provided by the Fleet Air Arm and then, on 24 April, eighteen Gloster Gladiators of Fighter Command's 263 Squadron from the carrier HMS *Glorious* landed on a frozen lake near Andalsnes, only to be wiped out by air attack. Fighting on the ground continued until the end of the month, when the British pulled out of Namsos and Andalsnes but reinforced their forces near Narvik. A British destroyer, a French destroyer and a Polish destroyer were sunk in this period.

The fighting in Norway was continuing when the storm burst on 10 May over the Western Front. The Wehrmacht attacked under the codename Operation Fall Gelb (Case Yellow), its strength consisting of 157 divisions backed by over 3,500 aircraft. The combined Anglo-French forces totalled 135 divisions with fewer than 2,000 aircraft, many of the latter being obsolescent French fighters. The attack came as no surprise to the Allies but the Blitzkrieg tactics of swiftly advancing Panzers with Stuka dive-bombers acting as their forward artillery had not been anticipated. At home, Prime Minister Neville

A destroyer of the Royal Navy cleaving through the waves and leaving a wake, photographed in the early months of the war for publicity purposes. The censors have modified the photograph by deleting the mast with its various aerials and D/F loop, and drawing in a false one. The high-mounted guns on the port side are also faked.

Author's collection

Chamberlain resigned and a new National Government was formed under Winston Churchill on 11 May.

The land and air battles which followed in the Low Countries and France do not form part of this narrative and it is sufficient to record that the British Expeditionary Force and some of the French forces fell back to Dunkirk from where, beginning on 27 May, over 224,000 men were rescued by the Royal Navy and the gallant armada of privately owned small ships which sailed from England. In these operations the Royal Navy lost 7 destroyers and a minesweeper, while the French lost 2 flotilla leaders and 5 destroyers. On 10 June Benito Mussolini, anxious to grab shares in the spoils of war when his senior partner was heading for victory, declared that Italy was at war with France and Britain.

Meanwhile, other catastrophes beset the Royal Navy. Two cruisers were sunk off Norway. Then, after the defeat in the West, the 27,000 British troops in the Narvik area had to be evacuated. Most of this was carried out without loss until 8 June when the aircraft carrier HMS *Glorious* and two screening destroyers were intercepted south-west of Narvik by the battleships *Scharnhorst* and *Gneisenau*. All three Royal Navy warships were sunk, taking with them almost all the crews as well as the remaining Hurricanes of the RAF's 46 Squadron and the Gladiators of 263 Squadron, which had landed on the carrier.

Less well-known than the 'miracle of Dunkirk', 114,000 more men were rescued from French ports further west, including British, French, Polish, Czech and Belgian troops. On 17 June the liner SS *Lancastria* was at anchor off St Nazaire, packed with over 5,000 escaping servicemen, when she was set on fire by Luftwaffe bombs and sank in 15 minutes. About 3,000 men were lost, in what was probably the worst maritime disaster of all time. The Royal Navy also had the depressing task of bringing to Britain 22,000 men, women and children from the Channel Islands before these were occupied by the Germans.

The last French resistance collapsed and the country signed an armistice on 22 June. It was partitioned, with Germany controlling most of the country, including all the northern and western coasts, leaving a rump for the French to govern from a new capital, the town of Vichy in central France. The humiliation of this proud and cultured people was complete.

Not even the most dismal Cassandra on the Allied side could have foreseen these cataclysmic defeats. Winston Churchill told the country that the Battle of France was over and the Battle of Britain was about to begin. The last bastion of democracy in the West faced the possibility of invasion and occupation by the most hideous dictatorship of modern times. Yet, even if Britain could withstand this onslaught, the War Cabinet foresaw another looming peril to the country's existence – the Battle of the Atlantic.

The Fairey Swordfish was the most famous of the Fleet Air Arm's torpedo-carrying aircraft in the Second World War. It first entered service with 825 Squadron in July 1936 and equipped thirteen squadrons by the outbreak of war, as the spearhead of the Royal Navy's air striking force. Powered by a Bristol Pegasus engine of 690hp, it had a combat range of about 400 miles, was armed with a single forward-firing machine-gun and another in the rear cockpit, and could carry either a torpedo or 1,500lb of bombs. In spite of its low speed and vulnerability to fast monoplane fighters, its crews performed truly remarkable exploits throughout the war. The example in this photograph is pre-war.

Courtesy of **Aeroplane**

The Supermarine Walrus, such as serial K8559 here, was an amphibian employed by both the RAF and the Fleet Air Arm for reconnaissance or air–sea rescue. First entering service in 1934, it was powered by a Bristol Pegasus VI pusher engine of 775hp and armed with two Vickers machine-guns. A later version could also carry depth-charges. Although the cruising speed was merely 95mph and the range was only about 500 miles, it gave sterling service throughout the Second World War. Aircrew gave it the indecorous nickname of the 'Shagbat'.

Author's collection

Girls of the Women's Royal Naval Service passing an F24 camera to a Fairey Swordfish of the Fleet Air Arm on a flying training exercise. They also tested wireless sets and other equipment.

Author's collection

This example of a Short Singapore III, serial K4580, was on the strength of Coastal Command's 209 Squadron from February 1936 to December 1938. Powered by two Rolls-Royce Kestrel IX tractor engines of 675hp coupled with twin pusher engines, it could carry a bomb-load of 2,000lb and was armed with three Lewis guns. Only nineteen of these flying boats remained in service at the outbreak of war and were considered obsolescent. Those in service in the UK were employed on training duties.

Author's collection

The Saro London entered service with Coastal Command in April 1936 and was also employed overseas. Powered by two Bristol Pegasus engines of 1,055hp, the flying boat could carry a bomb-load of 2,000lb, was armed with three Lewis machine-guns and had a normal range of about 1,100 miles. Thirty were built and some remained in squadron service until June 1940, employed on patrol duties searching for U-boats, blockade runners and armed raiders. This example from 202 Squadron, possibly serial K5260, was photographed on an exercise being 'rescued' by the destroyer HMS *Forester*.

Author's collection

Seventeen Supermarine Stranraer flying boats were built in Britain, first entering squadron service in April 1937. Powered by two Pegasus X engines of 875hp, they had a maximum range of about 1,350 miles, were armed with three Lewis guns and could carry 1,100lb of bombs. The last of those built in Britain were withdrawn from squadron service in April 1941, after being employed on patrol duties. In addition, forty Stranraers were built under licence in Canada, such as this example from 5 (BR) Squadron of the home-based RCAF photographed on 13 April 1941 while on patrol over the west coast. These Stranraers of the RCAF were also employed on escorting incoming and outbound Atlantic convoys to and from Halifax in Nova Scotia.

Bruce Robertson collection

The Short Sunderland, adapted from the C-class Empire flying boat, entered service with the RAF in June 1938. It soon became the pride of Coastal Command, although only a few were in service at the outbreak of the Second World War. The Sunderland I was powered by four Bristol XXII engines of 1,010hp, had a range of over 2,500 miles and could carry 2,000lb of anti-submarine bombs or depth-charges. Defensive armament consisted of a 0.303-inch Vickers gun in the bow, two more in dorsal positions and four 0.303-inch Browning guns in the stern turret. Later marks were so heavily armed that the Germans named the flying boat 'The Flying Porcupine'. Eventually 749 Sunderlands of various marks were built.

Author's collection

A corvette of the Royal Navy on escort duties in the North Atlantic, with members of the crew setting the fuses of depth-charges. Merchant vessels and a Sunderland of Coastal Command are in the background.

Author's collection

A transport vessel photographed from a Short Sunderland of Coastal Command while on convoy patrol.

Author's collection

The Fairey Albacore was a carrier-borne torpedo-bomber which first entered service with the Fleet Air Arm's 826 Squadron in March 1940. It was powered by a Bristol Taurus engine of 1,065hp and the armament consisted of a forward-firing Browning gun and a Vickers gun in the rear cockpit. It could carry a torpedo or 2,000lb of bombs. The crew compartment was enclosed and there were other improvements on the Fairey Swordfish, but many pilots preferred the older machine.

Author's collection

Admiral of the Fleet Sir A. Dudley F.R. Pound, First Sea Lord and Chief of Naval Staff from 19 June 1939 to 13 October 1943.

Author's collection

Admiral Sir Charles L. Forbes, Commander-in-Chief of the Home Fleet from 12 April 1938 to 18 December 1940.

Author's collection

Generaladmiral Erich Raeder (centre), Commander-in-Chief of the Kriegsmarine (German Navy) from 1938 to 30 January 1943, when he was replaced by Grossadmiral Karl Dönitz. The photograph was taken during a visit to Wilhelmshaven when his rank was Generaladmiral (no British equivalent) but he was appointed Grossadmiral (Admiral of the Fleet) in April 1939.

Jak P. Mallmann Showell collection

Grossadmiral Karl Dönitz with two of his staff officers. He succeeded Grossadmiral Erich Raeder as Commander-in-Chief of the German Navy on 30 January 1943, while retaining the position of Commander-in-Chief of the U-boat Arm which he had held from October 1939.

Author's collection

This Type IIC, *U-56*, was one of the smaller coastal U-boats, commissioned on 26 November 1938. Numbers on conning towers were removed at the beginning of the war. Hand-rails were also removed when the boats went to sea. This U-boat lasted for almost the entire war. It was finally sunk, while under the command of Oberleutnant zur See Joachim Sauerbier, in the latter part of April 1945 when at anchor at Kiel during the heavy raids made by RAF Bomber Command and the US Eighth Air Force.

U-Boot-Archiv, Cuxhaven-Altenbruch

The U-boat tender *Saar*, of 2,710 tons displacement, at Kiel with Flotilla Weddigen, which consisted of the small Type II coastal U-boats.

U-Boot-Archiv, Cuxhaven-Altenbruch

Part of a coastal convoy of twenty-four merchant vessels, mostly colliers. Such coastal convoys required continual protection by escort vessels of the Royal Navy and aircraft of Coastal Command and Fighter Command. This strained the resources available for the Atlantic convoys.

Author's collection

The British merchant ship *Heronspool*, of 5,203 tons, was torpedoed on 13 October 1939 by the Type VIIB *U-48* when about 500 miles west of Land's End. She was sailing from Swansea to Montreal with a cargo of about 8,000 tons of coal. All her crew survived.

U-Boot-Archiv, Cuxhaven-Altenbruch

The French merchant ship *Louisiane*, of 6,903 tons, was torpedoed in the early morning of 13 October 1939 when about 500 miles west of Land's End by the Type VIIB *U-48*, commanded by Kapitänleutnant Herbert Schultze. She was sailing from Antwerp to Havana with a general cargo of about 5,000 tons.

U-Boot-Archiv, Cuxhaven-Altenbruch

A lifeboat from the *Louisiane*, photographed from the Type VIIB *U-48*. Only one crew member was lost in the sinking.

U-Boot-Archiv, Cuxhaven-Altenbruch

MIGHTIER YET!

In ships, tonnage and gun-power, the Navies of the British Empire are the most powerful sea force in the world—and another million tons of British warships are building

The German merchant ship *Borkum*, of 3,670 tons, was captured on 18 November 1939 by the armed merchant cruiser HMS *California*, while en route from Rosario in Argentina to Hamburg with a cargo of grain. A British prize crew was put on board but the vessel was torpedoed on 23 November 1939 by the Type VIIA *U-31* before she could be taken into harbour. She caught fire and was abandoned, as shown in this air photograph, and drifted ashore. Subsequently, she was towed to Rosyth for scrap.

Author's collection

A Royal Navy minesweeper on coastal duties during the Battle of Britain. The quadruple Vickers machine-guns of 0.5-inch calibre were ineffective as anti-aircraft weapons.

Author's collection

The destroyer HMS *Antelope*, of 1,337 tons displacement, armed with four 4.7-inch guns and capable of 37 knots, photographed before being fitted with radar. She had a successful career as a convoy escort in the early months of the Battle of the Atlantic. On 5 February 1940 she sank the Type IXA *U-41*, and on 2 November 1940 sank the Type VIIA *U-31*. This was the second sinking for *U-31*, for on 11 March 1940 it was sunk in the Schillig Roads by Blenheim IV serial P4852 of Bomber Command's 82 Squadron, flown by Squadron Leader M.V. Delap. It was the first to be sunk by the RAF. It was raised by the Germans and recommissioned.

Author's collection

Members of an anti-aircraft gun crew serving on a British destroyer engaged on convoy escort duties in the
North Atlantic.

Author's collection

Anti-aircraft gunners on a trawler taken into service by the Royal Navy and fitted with armament for anti-
submarine patrols and escort duties. The twin Lewis guns are of a First World War pattern, behind a
makeshift shield.

Author's collection

A Loire 130 flying boat catapulted from the French battleship *Dunkerque*, of 26,500 tons displacement, engaged on convoy patrol in the early months of the war.

Author's collection

(*Above*) After seeking refuge in Montevideo, the main port of Uruguay, *Admiral Graf Spee* was scuttled. Clouds of black smoke rose as she sank. All the crew members were interned in Buenos Aires but their commander, Captain Langsdorff, committed suicide.

Author's collection

(*Opposite, top*) The *Leander* class cruiser HMS *Ajax*, flagship of the South Atlantic Squadron, made a goodwill visit to Montevideo after the successful action against the *Admiral Graf Spee*. She had a displacement of 6,985 tons, was armed with eight 6-inch guns, and was capable of 32 knots.

Author's collection

(*Opposite, bottom*) The crew of the cruiser HMS *Achilles*, which was manned by New Zealanders, made a triumphal march in Auckland after their successful action against the *Admiral Graf Spee*. The leading members of the crew in this photograph have passed under a banner with the words 'Rule! Rule! Britannia!'

Author's collection

Destroyers of the French Navy, photographed from a cruiser while ploughing through heavy seas in an early period of the war. The large destroyer flying the Tricolour appears to be a *contre-torpilleur* of the *Guépard* class, 2,436 tons displacement, which was armed with five 140-cm guns and capable of 35 knots.

Author's collection

The transfer of home mail from a destroyer to a larger warship, while both continue on their way. The photograph was taken in the early months of the war.

Author's collection

The Blackburn Skua was the first British aircraft designed as a fighter/dive-bomber, as well as the first monoplane to enter service with the Fleet Air Arm. In 1938, No. 800 Squadron on HMS *Ark Royal* received Skuas, fitted with Perseus XII engines of 890hp and armed with four 0.303-inch Browning machine-guns in the wings and a Lewis gun in the rear cockpit. The bomb-load was normally a single 500-pounder. A Skua from HMS *Ark Royal* shot down the first enemy aircraft of the war, in the North Sea, on 26 September 1939. This was Dornier Do18D-1 of 2. Staffel, Küstenfliegergruppe 106, and the four crew members were picked up by the destroyer HMS *Somali*.

Courtesy of Aeroplane

Turning into Wind by Charles J. Thompson GAvA, ASAA, GMA, EAA
Blackburn Skua serial L2885 of the Fleet Air Arm with HMS *Ark Royal*.

The German 'K' class cruiser *Königsberg*, of 6,650 tons displacement, was armed with nine 15-cm guns and was capable of 32 knots. She was damaged by shore batteries at Bergen on 9 April 1940, during the invasion of Norway. On the following day she was dive-bombed and sunk by Blackburn Skuas of the Fleet Air Arm's 800 and 803 Squadrons from Hatston in the Orkneys. Hit by several 500lb bombs, she was the first major warship to be sunk in wartime by air attack.

Author's collection

CHAPTER TWO

HAPPY TIME
FOR U-BOATS

O n 23 June 1940, the day after the French signed their armistice with Germany, a huge convoy of German trucks set out from Wilhelmshaven, loaded with all kinds of equipment required for the operation of U-boats. Two days later these German forces occupied the naval base and dockyard of Lorient in Brittany, overlooking the Bay of Biscay, which was destined to become part of Führer der Unterseeboote (West), the major command which fought the Battle of the Atlantic. The other French ports which were also occupied by the Germans and formed part of this command were Brest and St Nazaire in Brittany, together with Bordeaux, La Pallice and La Rochelle on the Atlantic coast.

Construction of great bomb-proof shelters for U-boats began in these ports but meanwhile most of the original docks could be used without delay. Kapitän-leutnant Fritz-Julius Lemp took his Type VII *U-30* into Lorient on 7 July to load torpedoes and prepare for another war cruise. The German U-boats would no longer have to pass from Kiel or Wilhelmshaven round the north of the British Isles to attack their objectives. Their route to the patrol area had been reduced by about 450 miles, so that a far greater proportion of their flotillas could be kept on patrol. Moreover, the ports of Bergen, Trondheim and Narvik were being prepared as part of Führer der Unterseeboote (Norway). In all, 25 U-boats had been lost since the beginning of the war but the number available for the battle had been built up to 51, of which 27 were ocean-going, while more replacements were under construction. The period which the crews later termed 'The Happy Time' was about to begin.

The Royal Navy under Admiral of the Fleet Sir Dudley Pound and the RAF's Coastal Command under Air Chief Marshal Sir Frederick Bowhill faced a situation that must have exceeded their worst nightmares. Germany's short coastline with the North Sea had been suddenly enlarged to one which stretched from the North Cape of Norway to the Franco-Spanish border. The British sea and air forces were incapable of maintaining an effective blockade over this vast expanse. The Home Fleet was engaged on measures to defend Britain's shores from an expected invasion while the main efforts of the RAF were necessarily concentrated on building up Fighter Command to combat the assault of the Luftwaffe. In addition, with Italy's entry into the war, a great new theatre had been opened up in the Mediterranean. Here the French warships would

The French battleship *Bretagne* of 22,200 tons displacement photographed on fire after bombardment by Royal Navy capital ships on 3 July 1940 while at Mers-el-Kebir in Algeria, to prevent her falling into German hands. In the foreground is her sister ship *Provence* and on the right is the battleship *Strasbourg* of 26,500 tons; both were scuttled by the French at Toulon on 27 November 1942.

Author's collection

constitute a new threat, if they were ordered by the Vichy government to fall in with the Third Reich. With a heavy heart, the Royal Navy was compelled to remove part of that threat by bombarding French warships at Mers-el-Kebir on 3 July 1940.

The British people, under the inspired leadership of their charismatic prime minister, seemed fully resolved to continue the war, in spite of the loss of almost all their Army's equipment in France. Hitler could not understand the intransigence of these obstinate people. His diplomatic overtures aimed at a peaceful settlement with Britain met with no response. His speech on 19 July in the Reichstag was directed at the British people, making 'A last appeal to reason'. When this was also rejected with amused contempt, the Luftwaffe began their operations against shipping in the Channel, intended to bring Fighter Command to battle and gradually wipe out a force which was erroneously believed to be only a fraction of its true size.

While the Luftwaffe and Fighter Command were locked in desperate combat in the skies over south-east England, a great invasion force of 250,000 men was being assembled and trained along the shores of northern France, under Operation Seelöwe (Sealion). These men were part of the victorious Wehrmacht, which had defeated the British Expeditionary Force and driven it back to its own country. Under the command of Feldmarschall Walther von Brauchitsch, they were to be carried across the Channel by a fleet of merchant ships, trawlers, barges, tugs and motor boats assembled by Grand Admiral Erich Raeder, who commanded the Kriegsmarine. As soon as the Luftwaffe had eliminated Fighter

Command, landings would take place between Folkestone and New Romney and between Hastings and Rye, with other smaller forces landing as far west as Brighton. Minefields would protect the flanks of this invasion force, while the Luftwaffe dropped a parachute division near Folkestone and dealt with any Royal Navy vessels that approached. From the bridgeheads on the English coast, the invasion force would sweep inland to London, spearheaded by Junkers Ju87 dive-bombers, and eventually would subjugate the whole of Britain.

Of course the RAF was fully aware of the dangers posed by the use of the French ports by U-boats and made photo-reconnaissance flights from the end of June. Small bombing attacks against the docks at Brest began on the night of 23/24 July. Wellingtons, Hampdens, Whitleys and Blenheims of Bomber Command were employed from this date, with Lorient becoming an additional target from 10/11 August. But only tiny numbers of aircraft were engaged on these tasks, while the main weight of Bomber Command was directed against targets in Germany and the invasion ports. They constituted no more than minor pinpricks to the occupying Germans and were only a shadow of the immense raids which followed in later years.

Thus the rejuvenated U-boat force was at work and it was time for Admiral Karl Dönitz to implement his tactics with renewed vigour. He knew that the maximum speed of his U-boats on the surface, about 18 knots, exceeded that of all escort vessels except destroyers. The latter were too few in number to escort all the convoys, especially when so many of them were required on home duties to help repel a possible invasion. On the other hand, a submerged U-boat crept along at a mere 4 knots at the most. Since Asdic was of little use against a U-boat on the surface, night attacks against convoys were vastly preferable, with the U-boat slipping through the inadequate escort screen time after time and then outrunning the pursuit. The low silhouettes of the U-boats were difficult to spot at night from convoy escorts or merchant vessels, especially when down-moon or in poor weather. The lookouts had to concentrate with their binoculars for long periods, often in conditions of pitching seas and numbing cold. The explosion of a torpedo against the hull of a merchant ship was frequently the first indication of the presence of their deadly enemy.

The record of Coastal Command against U-boats continued to be poor in this period, although its first sinking took place south-west of Ireland on 1 July 1940 when Sunderland I serial P9603 of 10 (RAAF) Squadron, flown from Mount Batten in Devon by Flight Lieutenant W.M. Gibson, attacked the Type IA *U-26*, commanded by Kapitänleutnant Heinz Scheringer. This U-boat had already been damaged by the corvette HMS *Gladiolus* and was trying to escape on the surface when Gibson made two attacks, each with four 250lb anti-submarine bombs. Scheringer scuttled his boat but forty-eight of his crew were rescued.

There were three home-based operational Groups in Coastal Command, No. 15 covering the south-west approaches of the North Atlantic and the western part of the Channel, No. 18 covering the north-west approaches of the North Atlantic and the southern area of the North Sea, and No. 16 operating over the eastern area of the Channel and the southern area of the North Sea. Overseas, the British had landed in Iceland on 10 May 1940, partly to prevent the Germans from using the island in their U-boat campaign and partly to provide bases for the Royal Navy and Coastal Command. Although the British presence was fairly benign it did not meet with the whole-hearted approval of the Icelanders, who not unnaturally valued their independence. However, Icelandic fjords could be used by flying boats and in August 1940 the RAF also began work on setting up an airfield under No. 18 Group. In addition, No. 200 Group at Gibraltar was transferred to Coastal Command on 12 August 1940, after the entry of Italy into the war, although initially it had only a single squadron on its strength.

Coastal Command was still extremely short of suitable aircraft, although more Sunderlands were being produced, Hudsons were steadily replacing Ansons and Beauforts had completely replaced the Vildebeests. There were, however, some glimmers of hope for an improved performance against U-boats. The drum-shaped Mark VII naval depth-charge of 450lb was modified in the summer of 1940. With a rounded fairing in the nose, fins in the rear and a hydrostatic pistol set to explode at a depth of 25 feet, the thin casing of this airborne depth-charge contained far more explosive, weight for weight, than the anti-submarine bomb. One disadvantage was that the weapon had to be dropped from a height of no more than 100ft and at a speed of no more than 115mph to prevent damage on hitting the water. Even then, depth-charges were seldom lethal unless they exploded within 15 feet of a U-boat.

The 450lb airborne depth-charge was a great improvement and work began on producing a 250lb version. The first time these new weapons were used effectively was not until 10 February 1941 when Whitley V serial P5050 of 502 Squadron, based at Limavady in Northern Ireland, damaged the Type VIIC *U-93* while escorting a convoy. The U-boat managed to return to Lorient.

Another new device that was to have far-reaching consequences was the Air to Surface-Vessel (ASV) radar, developed by the government's Telecommunications Research Establishment. This consisted of a small airborne transmitter and receiver capable of identifying a vessel on the surface and displaying the result on a cathode ray screen. Trials had begun in November 1939 with the ASV Mark I, on 214 megacycles frequency, but this early model proved less than effective. Its range was about 5 miles when the aircraft was at 3,000ft, but at this height the display was confused with echo signals from the sea's surface. Reception was far clearer at about 200ft, but the vessel could be picked up from only about half a mile. A few Hudsons were equipped with this new device in January 1940 but improvements needed to be made.

The new ASV Mark II, operating on 176 megacycles, with a more powerful transmitter and a more sensitive receiver, was duly devised and put into production for proposed delivery in August 1940. Unfortunately for Coastal Command, this was at a time when urgent efforts were devoted to producing an Airborne Interception (AI) radar for the RAF's night-fighters. This became an even greater necessity when the Luftwaffe, thwarted by its failure to defeat Fighter Command in the Battle of Britain, began heavy bombing attacks against London on the night of 7/8 September 1940, followed by attacks against ports such as Plymouth, Bristol and Liverpool. Some of the ASV transmitters destined for Coastal Command were converted for this purpose, and it was not until October 1940 that the first of the ASV Mark IIs became available, but there were still too few at this stage to equip all the anti-submarine aircraft. Their performance was enhanced by the installation of sideways-looking aerials in some machines. At the same time efforts were made to increase the number of radio-telephony sets available for the aircraft, to enable the crews to communicate directly with the Senior Naval Officers on the convoys. Hitherto, the normal method had been by Aldis lamp, wireless telegraphy and Morse, all of which were too slow and unsatisfactory for effective communication.

Another event soon afterwards was the creation of the Coastal Command Development Unit (CCDU). This was formed on 22 November 1940 at Carew

The Fairey Fulmar I was a carrier-borne two-seater with folding wings, employed by the Fleet Air Arm as a fighter from June 1940. Powered by a Rolls-Royce engine of 1,035hp, it was armed with eight Browning machine-guns in the wings. Its performance proved disappointing, owing to its considerable size and weight, with a lack of speed in level flight. This example is serial N1858, one of the pre-production prototypes.

Courtesy of Aeroplane

Cheriton in Pembrokeshire with a nucleus of skilled pilots and ground crews from 217 Squadron at St Eval in Cornwall (a Beaufort squadron which the author joined a few weeks later). The initial aircraft were an Anson, a Beaufort and a Hornet Moth, although a Whitley and a Hudson soon followed, with Wellingtons arriving later. One of the first tasks of this new unit was to test the new ASV Mark II under operational conditions, and this was followed by many other experiments which would have a dramatic effect on the efficiency of Coastal Command.

Meanwhile, the U-boats continued their massacre. On 17 August, when the Battle of Britain was at its height, Hitler had ordered the blockade of the British Isles and authorised the sinking of neutral ships. In the five months from the beginning of June to the end of October 1940, the U-boats sank 274 ships totalling 1,395,000 tons, at a loss of only six of their number in the North Sea. Of these six, two were sunk by warships, one by a combination of warships and the RAAF, one from striking a mine and two from unknown causes.

Another German weapon introduced to plague the Atlantic convoys was the Focke-Wulf Fw200C-1 Condor, a four-engined aircraft developed from a civil airliner. Based from August 1940 at Mérignac near Bordeaux as part of I./Kampfgeschwader 40, these long-range bombers could operate as far as 18 degrees west, beyond the range of RAF aircraft at the time. Their favourite targets were single ships or stragglers from convoys. Although they were able to carry only a fairly light bomb-load, four 550-pounders, the anti-aircraft defences of Allied merchant ships were almost non-existent in 1940. Guns had been mounted on about 1,500 of these ships by the end of 1939, but most were ancient weapons intended for defence against U-boats and capable of firing only at low elevation.

In the first two months of operating, the Condors sank thirty merchant vessels totalling 110,000 tons. Efforts were made by the British to improve defences against them. Some anti-aircraft guns were provided from shore establishments while arrangements for training volunteers to man them were put into force. The Maritime Anti-Aircraft Regiment of the Royal Artillery was formed, but it would be months before the merchant vessels had any reasonable security. Equally worrying for the British, the Condors frequently reported the exact position of convoys, enabling the U-boats to gather in 'wolf-packs' and pick off their victims at night.

The U-boats based in France were joined by twelve Italian submarines from 4 September 1940. These had sailed from La Spezia in Italy six days before and passed successfully through the Straits of Gibraltar to base themselves in Bordeaux under the name 'Betasom'. They came under the direction of Dönitz for their operations in the Atlantic, although he was not impressed with their performance at this stage. The area they were allotted initially was between the Azores and Spain, and then the North Channel around Ireland. The first of them to be sunk was *Commandante Faà di Bruno* on 8 November 1940, by the destroyer HMS *Havelock*. Nine more of these Italian submarines joined Betasom in November 1940, but by May 1941 their total number was reduced to ten, by sinkings or withdrawal to the Mediterranean theatre.

By the late summer of 1940 the homeward-bound convoys sailing across the North Atlantic were divided into two categories, the faster sailing from Halifax in Nova Scotia retaining the HX prefix while the slower, sailing from the port of Sydney in the north-east of the Canadian province, were given the prefix SC. As examples of the trials experienced by such convoys, it is recorded that the slower Convoy SC7, which left Sydney with 34 ships on 5 October 1940, lost 20 en route to U-boats, with 2 more damaged. The few escort vessels, hard-working and driven to desperation, were unable to sink any of the attackers. Then the faster Convoy HX79, which left Halifax with 49 ships and a more powerful escort a few days after SC7 left Sydney, suffered losses of 12 ships plus 2 others damaged. Once again, the U-boats escaped losses. The actions against these two convoys represented the first of the 'wolf-pack' tactics at night which Dönitz had long wished to employ. He had been unable to do so hitherto owing to a shortage of U-boats, but from this time wolf-packs were deployed whenever possible.

While these heavy losses were being incurred, officers in the Naval Intelligence Division of the Admiralty laboured to determine how many U-boats were in operation or under construction. They had discovered accurately the number operating at the beginning of the war, about fifty-seven, from documents recovered from the Type VIIB *U-49*, which had been sunk in Vaasfjord by British destroyers on 15 April 1940, during the Norwegian campaign. Information obtained from U-boat prisoners up to October 1940 indicated with some accuracy that about 30 U-boats had been lost since the beginning of the war but that 90 more had been commissioned. In fact the correct figure for new U-boats at the end of October was 98.

The centre of the Admiralty's anti-submarine war was the Submarine Tracking Room, known as NID 8(S) and staffed by about twelve people. A civilian who worked there from August 1940 was the barrister Rodger Winn, whose disability from poliomyelitis had prevented him taking any active part in the Royal Navy. Winn was appointed as its head at the end of 1940 and from that time made

Air Chief Marshal Sir Frederick W. Bowhill, the Air Officer Commanding-in-Chief of Coastal Command from 18 August 1937 to 14 June 1941.

Author's collection

some uncannily accurate guesses about the probable movements of U-boats. But at this stage decrypts of Kriegsmarine signals relating to U-boats were not yet forthcoming from the Government Code and Cypher School (GCCS) at Bletchley Park in Buckinghamshire, although it had succeeded in breaking the code used by the Luftwaffe. Certain inferences could be drawn from wireless telegraphy messages sent by the Kriegsmarine, picked up by the 'Y' Service already set up to intercept and record enemy signals, but these could not be decrypted.

By the end of October 1940 it was apparent that Hitler's plan to invade England had been shelved. The Luftwaffe had lost the battle in the air and the invasion fleet in the French ports was being dispersed. Some of the destroyers allocated to the defence of the east and south coasts of Britain could now be released to strengthen the slow corvettes and sloops which had been bearing the brunt of the Battle of the Atlantic. This brought immediate results with the sinking of three U-boats in November, but far more needed to be done. In September Churchill had managed to persuade President Roosevelt to release fifty American destroyers of First World War vintage, then being held in reserve, in return for facilities in British bases in the Caribbean. Forty-four of these were taken over by the Royal Navy and six by the Royal Canadian Navy; they were officially 'Town Class' destroyers but were generally known as 'four-stackers'. They were poorly armed, fitted with ancient engines and wallowed in the water. However, after being fitted with Asdic, they proved useful stopgaps until more modern escorts could be built.

Only a handful of U-boats operated from French ports in the last months of 1940. Their activities were somewhat curtailed by severe weather in the North Atlantic. But they ranged over longer distances and began to appear off the coast of Portugal and even off West Africa, sinking nine ships in these waters during December. Over 494,000 tons of merchant ships were sunk by U-boats, Condors and surface raiders in the North Atlantic during November and December, but only two U-boats were sunk.

The first surface raider to enter the North Atlantic during the winter was the pocket battleship *Admiral von Scheer*, which slipped round the north of Iceland and attacked Convoy HX84 on 11 November 1940. After sinking five merchant ships and the armed merchant cruiser *Jervis Bay*, she continued to the Indian Ocean and took a further heavy toll. With a total of about 99,000 tons to her credit, she succeeded in reaching home unscathed.

Then the heavy cruiser *Admiral Hipper* made an appearance in early December 1940. She tackled Convoy WS5A, making for the Middle East, but the escort proved too strong and she was slightly damaged. She headed for Brest and entered this haven on 27 December, to undergo repairs. The author's squadron, no. 217, was ordered to make a daylight attack on 1 February 1941 and dispatched six Beauforts; these were recalled owing to lack of cloud cover, but two aircraft were lost. The cruiser made another foray soon afterwards, sinking eight merchant vessels before returning once more to Brest. No. 217 Squadron was ordered to make another daylight attack on 15 February, and dispatched three Beauforts; all three were shot down by German fighters near the target. Undamaged by any air attack, the *Admiral Hipper* returned to Germany soon afterwards for a refit.

It was clear to the War Cabinet that wolf-pack attacks would intensify in the spring. Winston Churchill announced that the Battle of the Atlantic was the most serious problem faced by the country. On 6 March 1941 he issued a directive which gave top priority to combating the U-boat threat. Some action had already been taken. A new bomb-proof Operations Room had been set up during the previous month at Derby House in Liverpool, under the Admiral Commanding-in-Chief, Western Command. Coastal Command's 15 Group had moved there from Plymouth on 14 February, while the new 19 Group was formed to cover the area south of Ireland and the Bay of Biscay. A huge wallchart in this combined centre at Derby House showed the position of every convoy and their escorts, every Royal Naval warship in the Atlantic, all RAF aircraft on patrol and the reported positions of U-boats. Intelligence was obtained from the Admiralty in London, the two nerve-centres being connected by teleprinter.

While these developments were under way, a change of fortune took place in the North Atlantic. More escort vessels were being commissioned by the Royal Navy, of which one of the best-known was the Flower class corvette. This sturdy and reliable vessel had a maximum speed of only about 15 knots, but was being produced in large numbers and was capable of crossing the Atlantic without refuelling. In addition, a new form of seaborne radar, known as the Type 271, was being fitted to some of the warships. Although as yet imperfect, this radar helped the escorts keep station with convoys and also offered the possibility of detecting U-boats on the surface, thus supplementing the underwater Asdic. Yet another introduction was the 'Snowflake' rocket, designed to hang in the air and give a brilliant light which might enable the escorts to spot a U-boat, but this was not issued until the following May.

The Operations Room at Derby House in Liverpool, which on 14 February 1941 became the combined headquarters for waging the Battle of the Atlantic. It housed the Admiral Commanding-in-Chief, Western Command, and the Air Officer Commanding-in-Chief, 15 Group, together with their staffs. The Royal Navy and the RAF worked in close and effective collaboration.

Author's collection

In January and February 1941 over 531,000 tons of shipping had been sunk by U-boats and Condors in the North Atlantic, but no U-boats had been lost. This toll of merchant ship losses began to rise in March, but suddenly the escorts struck back. On 8 March 1941 the Type VIIB *U-47*, commanded by the legendary Kapitänleutnant Günther Prien, was sunk by HMS *Wolverine* while attacking Convoy OB293. Nine days later the escorts of Convoy HX112 sank two more U-boats. The Type VIIB *U-100* was rammed by the destroyer HMS *Vanoc* and its commander, Kapitänleutnant Joachim Schepke, was not among the few survivors. The destroyer HMS *Walker* accounted for the Type VIIB *U-99* on the same day and its commander, Fregattenkapitän Otto Kretschmer was taken prisoner. These three were ace commanders in the U-boat arm, and their loss was a grievous blow to Admiral Dönitz.

The Government Code and Cipher School at Bletchley Park continued its efforts to break the Enigma code used by U-boats. There were two keys, Home Waters and Foreign Waters, but the U-boats used the latter only in distant waters. One requirement was the capture of an Enigma machine and the code books for the Home Waters, provided this could be done in operations which did not arouse the suspicions of the Kriegsmarine. A Commando raid against the Lofoten Islands off the coast of Norway on 3 and 4 March 1941 provided valuable

On 3 March 1941 a Commando raid took place on the Lofoten Islands, off the coast of Norway, as a diversion for a combined operation against the island of Vaasgö south of Trondheim. Oil plants were put out of action, stocks set on fire, prisoners taken and numerous Norwegians brought back to serve in the British forces. One of the most important benefits was the discovery of a spare set of Enigma rotors on the armed trawler *Krebs*, which proved of great value to the cryptanalysts at the Government Code and Cipher School, Bletchley Park.

Author's collection

information when a spare set of Enigma rotors was discovered in the armed trawler *Krebs*, enabling the cryptanalysts to read the traffic for April and part of May 1941 and provide a basis for further decrypts.

The decryption indicated that the Kriegsmarine was operating a couple of weather ships in the North Atlantic and the Admiralty determined to capture these for intelligence purposes. The first was the *München*, north of Iceland, which was duly approached on 7 May by three cruisers and four destroyers. The German crew had sufficient time to jettison their Enigma machine and code books before the boarding party entered the radio room. The British found only a set of out-of-date papers in the officers' quarters, which proved of little value to Bletchley Park.

The real breakthrough came unexpectedly on 9 May, when the Type IXB *U-110*, commanded by Kapitänleutnant Fritz-Julius Lemp, and another U-boat attacked Convoy OB318 near Greenland. The escort commanders were surprised to experience an attack so far to the west. Two vessels were torpedoed before *U-110* was brought to the surface by depth-charges from the corvette HMS *Aubrietia*, commanded by Lieutenant-Commander F.V. Smith. Lemp ordered his boat to be scuttled and abandoned. The destroyer HMS *Bulldog* had turned on a ramming course when Commander A.J. Baker-Cresswell realised that a capture might be possible and instead ordered a whaler with a boarding party to be lowered. The U-boat men were in the water when Lemp ordered the watch officer to swim back with him to the boat. The German commander was never seen again but the watch officer was rescued with thirty-one other men.

The whaler reached the U-boat and the boarding party climbed inside, where they recovered a great deal of material from the control room. These included a three-wheel Enigma machine and, even more important, a set of code books. The U-boat was taken in tow by the *Bulldog*, with the intention of taking it to Iceland, but the weather worsened and it sank some hours later. The trophies were received with delight by the cryptanalysts at Bletchley Park.

While these event were taking place, another huge threat faced the British. The battleships *Scharnhorst* and *Gneisenau* (classed as battle cruisers by the Royal Navy) sank 115,622 tons of shipping within two months in the North Atlantic, before entering Brest on 21 March 1941. By this time the French port was the most heavily defended place in mainland Europe and the German battleships became prime targets for both Bomber Command and Coastal Command. They escaped damage until the night of 4/5 April when a bomb fell into the dry dock occupied by the *Gneisenau* but did not explode. The battleship was towed to the outer harbour where she was photographed by a reconnaissance Spitfire. Six Beauforts of 22 Squadron, on detachment at St Eval from North Coates in Lincolnshire, were ordered to attack. One of these, flown by Flying Officer Kenneth Campbell, found the battleship on the morning of 6 April in extremely poor weather and dropped a torpedo which blew a 40ft hole in her starboard side. Campbell was immediately shot down and killed, along with his three crew members, but the *Gneisenau* was out of commission for over five months.

Then the great German battleship *Bismarck*, one of the most powerful in the world, entered the North Atlantic. She left Gotenhafen on 19 May, commanded by Kapitän zur See Ernst Lindemann. Admiral Günther Lütjens was also on

On 7 April 2000, at Saltcoats in Ayrshire, the Victoria Cross awarded posthumously to Flying Officer Kenneth Campbell for his attack against the *Gneisenau* on 6 April 1941 was handed to 22 Squadron RAF in a ceremony organised by Ayrshire County Council. Left to right: Ron Bramley (one of the survivors of the crews of the six Beauforts of 22 Squadron dispatched on the attack); James Campbell, aged 91 (elder brother of Kenneth Campbell); Wing Commander David A. Simpson (Officer Commanding 22 Squadron); Bill Brady from South Africa (largely responsible for the occasion). The Campbell family gave the Victoria Cross to 22 Squadron in perpetuity, with the stipulation that it must be regarded as an award to all four members of the Beaufort crew killed in the attack.

Author's collection

board, ready to command the task force of the *Bismarck* and the heavy cruiser *Prinz Eugen*. The two warships joined up and sailed to Norway, where the battleship anchored at Grimstadtfjord with the cruiser nearby at Kalvanes Bay. They had been spotted en route by a Swedish cruiser and the information had been passed to the British through diplomatic channels. Two photo-reconnaissance Spitfires took off from Wick in Caithness on 21 May and one of these, serial X4496 flown by Flying Officer Michael F. Suckling, photographed the enemy warships only two hours after they anchored.

The British were already aware of the probable intentions of the Germans from their signals, even though at this time there was a delay of several days in decryption. Maryland I serial AR720 of the Fleet Air Arm, flown by Lieutenant Noel E. Goddard, was dispatched on the following day from Hatston in the Orkneys, and established that the *Bismarck* had left. Admiral Sir John Tovey, the commander of the Home Fleet, ordered battleships and cruisers to patrol the Denmark Strait, between Iceland and Greenland.

In the ensuing sea battle, on 24 May, a broadside from the *Bismarck* struck the battle cruiser HMS *Hood*, which blew up with a tremendous explosion. Only

The *Gneisenau* viewed from the starboard side. She was recorded as a battle cruiser by the British but classified as a battleship by the Kriegsmarine. Her length was 771ft and her displacement was 34,841 tons. The main armament consisted of nine 28-cm and 15-cm guns. Anti-aircraft armament included fourteen 10.5-cm, sixteen 3.7-cm and twelve 2-cm guns. She could achieve a speed of 32 knots.

Author's collection

three men from her complement of 1,419 survived. The battleship HMS *Prince of Wales* was damaged but three of her shells struck the *Bismarck*, causing a leak of oil and an inrush of sea water. This damage was observed by a Sunderland of 201 Squadron flown from Iceland by Flight Lieutenant Richard J. Vaughan, who reported it to a shadowing cruiser.

Admiral Lütjens signalled his decision to break off the sortie and make for St Nazaire. He detached the *Prinz Eugen* to Brest. Other British warships closed in and the aircraft carrier HMS *Victorious* dispatched 9 Swordfish and 5 Fulmars. The Swordfish scored one torpedo hit but caused little damage. Then the *Bismarck* managed to elude her pursuers until she was found at 10.30 hours on 26 May by Catalina serial AH545 of 209 Squadron, flown from Lough Erne in Northern Ireland by Pilot Officer Denis A. Briggs. This squadron had received the new flying boats only a few weeks before.

In the early afternoon of the same day 14 Swordfish from the aircraft carrier *Ark Royal* took off but in the extremely bad weather mistook the nearby cruiser HMS *Sheffield* for their target and attacked, fortunately without causing damage. In the early evening 15 Swordfish took off for another attack and this time found

A pre-war photograph of HMS *Ark Royal*, with Fairey
Swordfish serial L9781 above her.

Author's collection

the *Bismarck* – with dramatic results. Of the two torpedoes which struck home, one exploded on the port side of her stern, damaging the propellers, flooding the steering compartments and jamming the rudders in a position of 12 degrees to port.

The *Bismarck* could now steer only in a circle, and British battleships caught her in the early morning of 27 May. They pounded her until her guns were knocked out and the order to scuttle was given, but only 85 men from her complement of over 2,200 were rescued. Both Lindemann and Lütjens were killed. In his report Admiral Tovey paid tribute to their 'most gallant fight against impossible odds'. The British could not know that no other German heavy warships would enter the Atlantic during the war.

Two elderly battleships, the *Courbet* built in 1911 and the *Paris* built in 1912, arrived in England at the time of the fall of France. Both were of 22,189 tons displacement and identical in all major respects. One arrived at Plymouth and the other at Portsmouth. The British censor has blotted out the background of this photograph.

Author's collection

Marshal Henri Pétain, the leader of unoccupied Vichy France, and Admiral Jean Darlan, the commander of the remaining Vichy French Navy, on a visit to Toulon in order to inspect the battleship *Dunkerque* of 26,000 tons displacement, which was damaged during the bombardment of Mers-el-Kebir by the Royal Navy on 3 July 1940. She was scuttled by the French in November 1942 to prevent her falling into German hands.

Author's collection

The Grumman Martlet I was a version of the F4F-3 Wildcat carrier-borne fighter employed by the US Navy. It was powered by a Wright R-1820 engine of 1,240hp and armed with four 0.50-inch machine-guns. France ordered a hundred of these machines but most of the contract was transferred to Britain and reached the Fleet Air Arm in July 1940. This example is serial AL257.

Author's collection

Blindfolded German prisoners being brought ashore at a port on the east coast of England, following an action in the early morning of 28 September 1940 when a motor launch of the Royal Navy rammed and set on fire an E-boat of the Kriegsmarine.

Author's collection

One of the destroyers provided for Britain by the USA, the USS *Abel P. Upshar* is seen here leaving port for service with the Royal Navy. Able seamen are securing a griping spar into position.

Author's collection

The *Deutschland* class heavy cruiser *Admiral von Scheer*, of 12,700 tons displacement, was known as one of the pocket battleships. She left Brunsbüttel on 27 October 1940 under the command of Kapitän zur See Theodor Krancke for a war cruise as a surface raider. After passing through the Denmark Strait into the North Atlantic, she attacked the homeward-bound convoy HX84 on 11 November and sank 5 of the 37 merchant ships. These were gallantly defended by the armed merchant cruiser *Jervis Bay*, which was also sunk. The *Admiral von Scheer* moved on to the South Atlantic and then to the Indian Ocean, where she operated with the armed merchant cruiser *Atlantis*, commanded by Kapitän zur See Bernhard Rogge. When she finally reached Kiel on 1 April 1941, she had sunk sixteen merchant ships totalling 99,059 tons. The *Atlantis* was sunk by the cruiser HMS *Devonshire* on 22 November 1941 and the *Admiral von Scheer* was hit and capsized at Kiel during a raid by Bomber Command on the night of 9/10 April 1945.

Jean-Louis Roba collection

A British tanker, torpedoed and sinking off Iceland in early 1941.

Author's collection

The heavy cruiser *Admiral Hipper*, of 13,900 tons displacement, was
armed with eight 20.3-cm guns and could achieve a speed of
32 knots. She was photographed on 20 January 1941 in dry dock
at Brest by a Spitfire of No. 1 Photographic Reconnaissance Unit
from St Eval in Cornwall. The warship had entered the French
port with machinery defects and slight damage from British
cruisers after commerce raiding in the Atlantic. She was scuttled in
Kiel Bay on 3 May 1945, after having been badly damaged by
Bomber Command on the night of 9/10 April 1945.

Author's collection

A study of a destroyer of the Royal Navy at high speed.

Author's collection

The U-boat ace commander Kapitänleutnant Günther Prien, whose Type VIIB U-47 torpedoed and sank the veteran battleship HMS Royal Oak, of 29,150 tons displacement, at Scapa Flow in the early morning of 14 October 1939, with the loss of 786 men. After a successful career in the North Atlantic, Prien was killed in the same U-boat when it was depth-charged and sunk early on 8 March 1941 by the destroyer HMS Wolverine, which was escorting convoy OB293. There were no survivors from the crew.

Author's collection

Far Left: Kapitänleutnant Joachim Schepke, one of the early U-boat ace commanders, was lost on 17 March 1941 when his Type VIIB U-100 was rammed in darkness by the destroyer HMS Vanoc, escorting convoy HX112 in the North Atlantic. Although the destroyer stopped and picked up seven survivors, Schepke was not among them.

Author's collection

Left: Fregattenkapitän Otto Kretschmer, the top scorer of the U-boat commanders, was captured on 17 March 1941 when his Type VIIB U-99 was wrecked by depth-charges fired by the destroyer HMS Walker, escorting convoy HX112 in the North Atlantic. Kretschmer and other survivors came to the surface and were picked up by the destroyer.

Author's collection

Flak over Brest photographed with a short time exposure on the night of 4/5 May 1941 by a Wellington IC of 115 Squadron based at Marham in Norfolk. Photo-interpreters identified (1) a flak battery; (2) tracer from light flak; (3) fogging caused by searchlights. At the time Brest was the most heavily defended place on mainland Europe.

Author's collection

A Mark XII torpedo being wheeled to a Beaufort I fitted with a blister gun under the navigator's position in the nose of the aircraft.

Author's collection

Flying Officer Kenneth Campbell. He was awarded a posthumous Victoria Cross after torpedoing and severely damaging the *Gneisenau* in the outer harbour at Brest. His aircraft, Beaufort serial N1016, was shot down immediately after the torpedo was released and all four crew members were killed.

Author's collection

The battleship *Gneisenau* in dry dock at Brest in 1941 for repairs to the damage caused by the torpedo dropped by Flight Lieutenant Kenneth Campbell of 22 Squadron on 6 April 1941. Water is being pumped out of her starboard quarter.

Jean-Louis Roba collection

Admiral Günther Lütjens was born in 1890 and entered the Imperial German Navy in 1907. He served in torpedo-boats in the First World War. By the outbreak of the Second World War he was Vice-Admiral in charge of reconnaissance forces in the North Sea. He was promoted to Admiral of the Fleet in September 1940 and gained operational experience in his flagship *Scharnhorst*. Although intelligent and courageous, he had a reserved and forbidding manner. He was killed on the *Bismarck*, shortly before she sank on 27 May 1941.

Author's collection

The battleship *Bismarck*, of 41,700 tons displacement, photographed from the heavy cruiser *Prinz Eugen* before sailing from Korsfjord in Norway for the North Atlantic. Her heavy armament consisted of eight 38-cm and twelve 15-cm guns, and she could achieve a speed of 29 knots.

Author's collection

Two Beaufort Is of 217 Squadron, bearing the squadron code letters MW, carrying torpedoes. Both survived operational careers. Aircraft letter E serial L4487 was struck off charge with No. 5 Operational Training Unit on 27 July 1944. Aircraft letter B serial N1019 was struck off charge with No. 51 Operational Training Unit on 15 November 1944.

Imperial War Museum TR31

The crew of a Bristol Beaufort I of 217 Squadron at RAF St Eval in mid-1941. Left to right: Sergeant Davies, wireless operator; Flying Officer Jack Percival, pilot; Sergeant Kenneth Reeves, air gunner; Pilot Officer Roy C. Nesbit, navigator and bomb aimer.

Author's collection

The Bristol Beaufort first entered service with Coastal Command in November 1939. With a crew of four, the Mark I was powered by two Taurus VI engines of 1,065hp and could carry up to 2,000lb of bombs or a single torpedo. The armament consisted initially of a single forward-firing machine-gun in the wing and another in the power-operated turret, but was gradually increased. It was a robust aircraft, although difficult to fly on one engine. It suffered the highest loss rate of all aircraft in the RAF during the Second World War, owing to its point-blank attacks at low level when carrying either a torpedo or bombs. This example is serial W6537 of 22 Squadron, the first to be fitted with seven guns.

C.H. Barnes via Roger Hayward

The battleship *Bismarck* and attendant vessels, photographed at Grimstadtfjord in Norway on 21 May 1941 by Flying Officer Michael F. Suckling of No. 1 Photographic Reconnaissance Unit.

Author's collection

The heavy cruiser *Prinz Eugen*, with destroyers and auxiliary vessels, photographed at Kalvanes Bay in Norway on 21 May 1941 by Flying Officer Michael F. Suckling of No. 1 Photographic Reconnaissance Unit.

Author's collection

Flying Officer Michael F. Suckling of No. 1 Photographic Reconnaissance Unit, who photographed the *Bismarck* and *Prinz Eugen* in Norwegian fjords on 21 May 1941, after taking off from Wick in Spitfire PR IC serial X4496. He lost his life on a photographic sortie over La Pallice exactly two months later.

Author's collection

Spitfire PR IB serial N3117, which was unarmed but fitted with an extra 29-gallon fuel tank behind the pilot. The PR IC serial X4496 in which Flying Officer Michael F. Suckling photographed the *Bismarck* and *Prinz Eugen* was additionally fitted with a 30-gallon blister tank under the port wing, counterbalanced by a blister housing two F-24 cameras under the starboard wing. This extra fuel enabled the machine to cover targets in Kiel and Norway.

Author's collection

Bismarck – into Battle by Mark Postlethwaite GAvA
The battleship *Bismarck* leaving Grimstadtfjord near Bergen on 21 May 1941, escorted by two Messerschmitt Bf110C-4s of Zerstörergeschwader 76 from Herdla, to join the heavy cruiser *Prinz Eugen* and begin her doomed foray into the North Atlantic.

Admiral Sir John C. Tovey, Commander-in-Chief of the Home Fleet from 22 December 1940 to 14 April 1943.

Author's collection

Quadruple 0.5-inch anti-aircraft guns on the Kent class cruiser HMS *Suffolk*, of 9,800 tons displacement, on patrol in the Arctic as part of the First Cruiser Squadron. Note the ice floes in the background. She was armed with eight 8-inch guns and could achieve 31 knots. At 19.22 hours on 23 May 1941 a lookout on this warship was the first seaman of the Royal Navy to spot the battleship *Bismarck* at sea, about 55 miles north-west of Iceland's North Cape.

Author's collection

A low-level reconnaissance photograph of the port of St Nazaire. The dry dock shown diagonally at top right was the only one on the west coast of France capable of accommodating battleships. The *Bismarck* headed for this port but never reached it.

The Consolidated Catalina I first entered service with Coastal Command's 240 Squadron in March 1941, based at Stranraer in Wigtownshire, followed later in the month by 209 Squadron at Lough Erne in Co. Fermanagh. Powered by two Pratt & Whitney R1830 Twin Wasp engines of 1,200hp, it was armed with a machine-gun in the bow, two in each of the side blisters, and another in a ventral position. It could carry a load of 2,000lb and had a normal range of about 2,000 miles.

Author's collection

Catalina serial AH545 of 209 Squadron at Lough Erne in Northern Ireland. This was the flying boat in which Pilot Officer Denis A. Briggs and his crew located the battleship *Bismarck* in the North Atlantic, at 10.30 hours on 26 May 1941, when about 690 miles west-north-west of Brest.

Author's collection

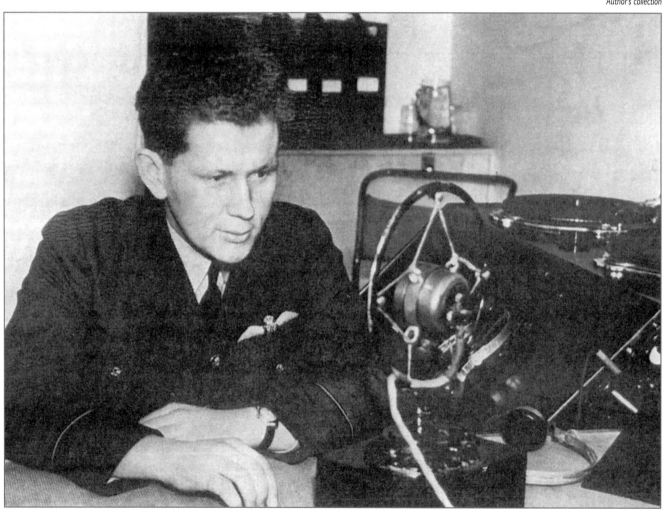

Flying Officer Denis A. Briggs, the captain of Catalina I, letter Z, serial AH545 of 209 Squadron based at Lough Erne in Northern Ireland, which located the battleship *Bismarck* in the North Atlantic at 10.30 hours on 26 May 1941. He was photographed during a BBC broadcast to the British public.

Author's collection

Two major warships which were part of Force H from Gibraltar ordered to intercept the *Bismarck*. The battle cruiser HMS *Renown* (left), of 30,750 tons displacement, was armed with six 15-inch guns and could achieve a speed of 30 knots. The aircraft carrier HMS *Ark Royal* astern of her had a displacement of 22,000 tons, could carry up to sixty aircraft and had a maximum speed of 31 knots.

Author's collection

The battleship HMS *King George V*, of 36,700 tons displacement, ploughing through heavy seas in the North Atlantic. She was armed with ten 14-inch and sixteen 5.25-inch guns and could achieve a speed of 28 knots.

Author's collection

The battleship HMS *King George V* firing quadruple 14-inch guns from her aft turret.

The *Nelson* class battleship HMS *Rodney*, of 36,000 tons displacement, firing a broadside from her nine 16-inch turret guns. In addition to this armament, she had twelve 6-inch guns. She could achieve a speed of 23 knots.

The battleship *Bismarck* carried four of these Arado Ar196A floatplanes for reconnaissance, spotting, liaison with friendly forces and fighter protection with their two machine-guns. They were housed in hangars near the mainmast and launched by means of a catapult. Powered by a BMW 132K radial engine of 970hp, the Ar196A had a range of about 650 miles. One attempted to take off from the *Bismarck* with the Fleet War Diary on 26 May 1941, when the battleship was about 450 miles west of Brest and warships of the Royal Navy were closing in, but the catapult was found to have been damaged.

Georges van Acker collection

An Arado Ar196A-3 of 2./Bordfliergerstaffel 196. Originally designed as a shipborne aircraft, the A-3 variant was employed on sea patrols from coastal bases, mostly over the Bay of Biscay and from islands in the Mediterranean.

Jean-Louis Roba collection

Survivors from the battleship *Bismarck* being rescued by the cruiser HMS *Dorsetshire* on 27 May 1941. Only 115 men were saved from her complement of over 2,200.

Author's collection

CHAPTER THREE

ALLIES FOR BRITAIN

In the three months from April to June 1941, 171 merchant ships totalling more than 903,000 tons were lost in the North Atlantic, with the rate of attrition rising steadily. Only seven U-boats were sunk in these months while the number on patrol continued to mount. The area of the conflict in the North Atlantic had spread westward and was being fought on a larger scale. Churchill's earlier fears that the U-boat war would be intensified in the spring had been realised. However, the number of naval escort vessels had also increased, as well as the aircraft on the strength of Coastal Command. Their weaponry was improving, while British Intelligence had made some extraordinary advances.

In this period the United States Navy became increasingly involved in the Western Atlantic. On 2 October 1939 the USA and other American republics had declared a 'Security Zone', covering the US eastern seaboard to 60 degrees west and then swinging southwards to cover the seaboard of Brazil as far as 20 degrees north. These waters were patrolled by US warships and the U-boats could not attack without the risk of drawing America into the war. Then, on 11 April 1941, the Americans moved this Security Zone eastward to 26 degrees west, inhibiting the U-boats from making attacks within a great swathe of the North Atlantic. In the meantime the Lease-Lend Act in the USA permitted the transfer of ten coastguard cutters to Britain. Arrangements were also made whereby warships of the Royal Navy could be repaired and refitted in American ports. Another move came in July 1941 when the Americans set up bases in Iceland and began to relieve the British troops from the task of garrisoning the country, even though the Icelanders continued to resent the presence of foreign 'invaders'. The USA was moving closer to active participation in the war against Germany, although the employment of her warships as convoy escorts in the North Atlantic had not yet begun.

The Royal Canadian Navy became stronger in this period, having grown from a nucleus of twelve small ships on the outbreak of war. New corvettes, built in Canada on the lines of the Royal Navy's Flower Class, were commissioned in April 1941, with many more under construction. By the end of May the Royal Canadian Navy was able to undertake escort duties in the Western Atlantic, even though its new recruits still lacked practical experience in the rigours of life in those turbulent waters. The Royal Navy was happy to hand over these duties to its naval comrades in the Dominion.

A sentry on board a coastal patrol vessel off the shores of Iceland. The Icelanders were unfriendly towards the British forces occupying their country. It was not considered a favoured posting by servicemen.

Author's collection

A momentous event on the world stage determined much of the course of the war and eventually affected the Battle of the Atlantic. On 10 May 1941 the Luftwaffe's Blitz on London and other cities had suddenly tailed off. The British had suspected for many months that Hitler would turn against Russia as soon as he had achieved all he could in the West. They knew from decrypts of enemy signals that many units of the Luftwaffe had been withdrawn to support a great build-up of German armies in the East. Churchill's warnings to Stalin went unheeded, as did those of the British ambassador in Moscow, Sir Stafford Cripps. Stalin was deeply suspicious of Britain's intentions and veracity, knowing nothing definite of her ability to decrypt German signals. When Operation Barbarossa began on 22 June 1941 and the advance of the Wehrmacht over the Russian plains towards Moscow seemed unstoppable, the need to supply arms by sea to Britain's new ally became apparent. The resources of both the Royal Navy and Coastal Command were to be strained even further.

Nevertheless the Battle of the Atlantic reached a stalemate in the summer of 1941. Although by this time about eighty operational U-boats were available to intensify the conflict, these found far fewer pickings. In the two months of July and August 1941 the rate of losses in the North Atlantic dropped to 84 merchant ships totalling about 181,000 tons, while four U-boats were lost. The U-boats were simply failing to make contact with the convoys. Much of the answer lay, of course, in the decrypts of signals at Bletchley Park which enabled the Submarine Tracking Room and the commanders at Derby House in Liverpool to route the convoys around the positions of waiting U-boats.

This phenomenon puzzled Dönitz, who suspected that the Royal Navy was somehow acquiring knowledge of U-boat locations, but he was assured by German experts that breaking into the codes was impossible. One other possible factor was the loss of several of his experienced commanders in the earlier months of 1941. These were men who had joined the Kriegsmarine before the war and combined technical knowledge, skill and determination to a greater degree than many of their younger successors. It can be shown statistically that 2 per cent of U-boat commanders sank almost 30 per cent of Allied shipping, whereas other commanders sank fewer and some none at all.

The British escort commanders, who were not privy to the secrets of Bletchley Park, believed that the explanation for the improved intelligence lay in the introduction of high-frequency direction-finding in their ships. These short-wave transmissions gave the bearings of U-boats when they sent signals, as they did on frequent occasions, to their command centre. Two or more bearings from different angles gave the position of a U-boat and enabled the convoy to steer clear of it. The Royal Navy called their HF/DF equipment 'Huff-Duff' and were very pleased with its performance. No doubt it was successful on occasions, but it was the decryptions of signals sent to and from the U-boats which were also responsible.

There were a few other flashes of light to relieve the gloom of these 'dark days', as Churchill called them. On 13 June 1941 the pocket battleship *Lützow*, renamed from *Deutschland* on Hitler's orders, was torpedoed off the south-west coast of Norway by a Beaufort of 42 Squadron, flown from Leuchars by Flight Sergeant Ray H. Loveitt, and was put out of action for a considerable period. Then the cruiser *Prinz Eugen*, which had arrived in Brest after her foray with the battleship *Bismarck*, was hit on the night of 1/2 July 1941 by a bomb dropped during a raid by fifty-two Wellingtons of Bomber Command. This bomb exploded inside her hull, killing sixty-one of her crew and putting her out of action for three months. The battleship *Scharnhorst*, which had been under repair in Brest for months after arriving at the port from her foray in the Atlantic, sailed south to La Pallice on 23 July 1941 for proving trials. But Bomber Command found her in a daylight raid on the following day and hit her with five bombs. She returned to Brest badly damaged and requiring four more months of repair. The prospect of further forays by German capital ships into the Atlantic receded, at least for the time being.

Measures were taken to reduce the depredations wrought by the Focke-Wulf Fw200 Condors. One idea was to launch 'expendable' RAF Hurricanes from merchant vessels to defend the convoys. The pilots, who were regarded as somewhat less expendable than their machines, could be either rescued from the sea or they could make for dry land after tackling the enemy. Curious as it may seem, there was no shortage of RAF volunteers for this apparently suicidal task. These pilots were trained at the Merchant Ship Fighter Unit (MSFU) at Speke near Liverpool, while Catapult-Aircraft Merchantmen (CAM-ships) were fitted with catapults to launch RAF Hurricanes converted for sea duties. Six of these CAM-ships were sailing with convoys by the end of June 1941, with many more under conversion.

The first 'kill' of a Condor by a Sea Hurricane occurred on 2 August 1941, not from a CAM-ship but from the 'fighter catapult ship' HMS *Maplin*. This

The Focke-Wulf Fw200 Condor was adapted from a passenger airliner to serve as a long-range anti-shipping bomber, and first entered service with Kampfgeschwader 40 at the end of 1940. The Fw200C-3 version shown here entered service in the summer of 1941. It was powered by four Bramo BMW 323R-2 engines of 1,200hp, was armed with five machine-guns and a 20-mm cannon, and could carry 2,100kg of bombs. The Condor achieved many successes against British shipping and became known as the 'scourge of the Atlantic'.

Author's collection

launched one of these aircraft, flown by Lieutenant Robert W.H. Everitt of the Fleet Air Arm, while sailing to meet an inward-bound convoy from Sierra Leone. After a long air battle Everitt set the enemy bomber on fire and it crashed into the sea. The Hurricane was also hit and Everitt ditched the machine, fortunately being picked up by an escorting destroyer. He was awarded the DSO. Another fighter catapult ship, HMS *Springbank*, was torpedoed and sunk west of Ireland on 27 September 1941, but these vessels and the CAM-ships had a deterrent effect on the Condors. They also scored successes against Junkers Ju88 bombers when escorting convoys to Russia in 1942.

August 1941 ended with a bizarre incident in the North Atlantic. The Type VIIC *U-570*, commanded by Kapitänleutnant Hans-Joachim Rahmlow, was unlucky enough to come to the surface in the morning of 27 August within sight of a Hudson of 269 Squadron, on patrol from Iceland with Squadron Leader James H. Thompson at the controls. The men on the conning tower did not spot the danger in time. Thompson dived and dropped four 250lb depth-charges on the crash-diving U-boat. These shattered instruments and damaged the batteries, causing chlorine gas to start filling the U-boat. Unlike most of his crew, Rahmlow was an experienced commander. He was forced to order the diving tanks to be blown, and the U-boat shot back to the surface.

One of the crew waved a white scarf at the Hudson, indicating surrender. Others released rubber dinghies, which were washed overboard and prevented any evacuation of the wounded. The diesel engines could not be started and Rahmlow decided to surrender and eventually scuttle the boat. He ordered all the

On 27 August 1941 a Hudson of 269 Squadron, flown by Squadron Leader J.H. Thompson from Kaldadarnes in Iceland, depth-charged the Type VIIC *U-570*, commanded by Kapitänleutnant Hans-Joachim Rahmlow, about 150 miles to the south. The explosions extinguished the lights in the U-boat and set off a discharge of chlorine gas. Some of the crew scrambled out of the conning tower and waved a white shirt as a token of surrender. Thompson waited until Catalina serial AH553 of 209 Squadron, flown by Flying Officer E.A. Jewiss, arrived from Reykjavik to continue circling.

Author's collection

Ships of the Royal Navy and the Royal Canadian Navy arrived but the seas were too rough to launch boats and board the U-boat. Relays of aircraft kept station during the short hours of darkness. This photograph shows the destroyer HMCS *Niagara* (formerly the USS *Thatcher*) near *U-570*.

Author's collection

When the sea calmed sufficiently, Lieutenant H.B. Campbell of the trawler HMS *Kingston Agate* crossed over in a life-raft and accepted surrender. The U-boat was towed to Iceland and made seaworthy for a voyage to Britain, where it was commissioned as HMS *Graph*. Although the code books had been destroyed and no intelligence was available for Bletchley Park, some information regarding practical aspects of German U-boats was gathered.

Author's collection

secret instruments and code books to be destroyed and awaited the Royal Navy, which duly arrived. Unfortunately for Rahmlow, the boarding party prevented the scuttling and took the U-boat in tow to Iceland. It was moved eventually to Britain and commissioned as HMS *Graph*, but the Enigma machine and the code books had been thrown overboard and the episode offered few advantages to Bletchley Park.

The British mounted a minor diversionary action at the end of August, when two cruisers and several destroyers escorted the liner *Empress of Canada*, carrying Canadian and other troops to raid the island of Spitzbergen. This was intended to deny facilities in this Arctic region to German U-boats but it also played on Hitler's fears that a larger attack would be made against the mainland of Norway and thus create another front for the forces of the Wehrmacht. The raid ended successfully on 3 September, but of course was little more than a pinprick to the Kriegsmarine.

Thwarted by the failure of his U-boats to achieve their normal level of sinkings in July and August, Dönitz assumed that their patrol lines were in the wrong positions and in September sent them to the south of Greenland. As it happened, this move coincided with alterations made in references in the Kriegsmarine's naval grid, causing some delay at Bletchley Park while the cryptanalysts worked out the new code letters. The wolf-packs closed in on Convoy SC42, which had sailed from Sydney in Nova Scotia on 30 August with 62 ships. They sank 16 of these in a protracted sea battle, for the loss of 2 U-boats, the Type IXC *U-501* sunk on 10 September by the corvette HMCS *Moosejaw* and the Type VIIC *U-207* sunk the following day by depth-charges dropped by 4 escorts. These sinkings contributed to a rise in total sinkings in September of 51 merchant vessels in the North Atlantic, totalling over 184,000 tons. Only the two U-boats listed above were sunk in that month.

The Battle of the Atlantic continued into October, with American participation becoming more marked. Already in September four US destroyers had formed part of the escort of Convoy HX150, which had left Halifax on 16 September and made the passage undisturbed by U-boats. A more serious episode occurred in mid-October when calls for help from Convoy SC48 resulted in a re-inforcement which included five US destroyers. By this time Dönitz had ordered his commanders to concentrate on the escorts and the USS *Kearney* was hit by a torpedo, killing eleven of her crew and injuring many others. She managed to reach Iceland, but another attack on 31 October resulted in even more serious consequences. On this occasion five US destroyers were escorting Convoy HX156 eastwards when the USS *Reuben James* was sunk by a torpedo fired by the Type VIIC *U-562*. She went down with 115 of her crew, only 45 men being rescued. Almost immediately, Congress revised the Neutrality Act to enable Roosevelt to order a more active role against U-boats, but soon afterwards the Americans decrypted Japanese signals indicating that the threat of war in the Pacific was looming. The USA did not possess sufficient naval forces to cope with wars in two oceans.

The U-boats sank 32 vessels totalling over 154,000 tons in the North Atlantic during October 1941, and it seemed inevitable that this rate of attrition would continue. But then, as so often in the war, Hitler's ineptitude as supreme commander of German forces came to the rescue of the hard-pressed Allies. On 22 November he ordered all operational U-boats in the Atlantic to move to the Mediterranean or the approaches to the Straits of Gibraltar. This order was given after the launch of a British offensive in the Western Desert on 18 November

Canadian servicemen arriving by liner at a British port after crossing the Atlantic. The contingent included a number of American volunteers, before their country had entered the war.

Author's collection

under the codename Operation Crusader, which in turn followed the destruction by the Royal Navy of all seven merchant vessels in an Axis convoy intended to supply the Deutsches Afrika Korps under General Erwin Rommel. The Axis forces, desperately short of fuel and other supplies, were making a fighting retreat.

Hitler's order put an end to operations by U-boats in the middle and west of the Atlantic for almost seven weeks, and availed little in their new areas. No fewer than 15 U-boats were sunk in all theatres during November and December 1941, while Allied losses in the Atlantic dropped to 20 ships totalling almost 101,000 tons. One of the major actions took place with Convoy HG76, consisting of 32 ships which left Gibraltar on 14 December bound for Britain with a very strong escort of 16 warships. The latter included Commander F.J. Walker in command of the sloop HMS *Stork* and the 36th Escort Group. Walker had specialised in anti-submarine warfare during the interwar period and was to become a legendary figure in the Battle of the Atlantic as the most successful group commander in the Royal Navy.

Convoy HG76 had to run the gauntlet of a wolf-pack lying in wait as well as attacks from Fw200 Condors based at Bordeaux. Air cover was available from Gibraltar for the first three days but thereafter the vessels depended on Grumman Martlets of the Fleet Air Arm from the escort carrier HMS *Audacity*, until they reached the protection of long-range Liberators based in Britain. The battle that ensued began three days later and continued for six days. In the course of the passage of this convoy, two Condors were shot down and several others driven off, although on 21 December HMS *Audacity* was torpedoed and sunk, as was the escort destroyer HMS *Stanley* and one of the merchant ships. But three U-boats were sunk and others attacked. Tactics developed by Commander Walker were employed, with the escorts working in concert and dropping patterns of depth-charges on the positions of U-boats picked up by Asdic. The wolf-packs were swamped by superior forces. The price was too heavy for Dönitz, who called off further attacks when the first Liberator appeared.

This was the month when the Second World War became truly global. On 7 December carrier-borne aircraft of the Japanese Navy attacked the US naval base at Pearl Harbor in Hawaii. Japan and the USA were at war, and Hitler was unwise enough to declare war on the USA four days later. At first, the Japanese seemed all-conquering. They swept down the Malayan Archipelago, sank the battleships HMS *Prince of Wales* and HMS *Repulse*, captured Singapore, conquered Hong Kong, overcame the Philippines and the Dutch East Indies, entered Borneo and occupied many islands in the Pacific. But there was no doubt in the minds of the Allied supreme commanders that in the end their democracies would prevail.

On 27 December the British mounted their first combined operation when the Royal Navy landed Commandos on the Norwegian islands of Vaasgö and Maalöy near Bergen, while the RAF bombed the nearby fighter airfield of Herdla. In spite of some losses, the raid was rated as a success, with merchant ships totalling 16,650 tons sunk, the German garrisons overcome, many installations destroyed and Norwegian volunteers brought back to join the armed forces. Perhaps even more important, it reinforced Hitler's erroneous belief that the British intended to launch a full-scale invasion of Norway.

At the same time the Chiefs of Staff approved the first major deception plan aimed at Hitler's credulity and belief in his intuitive powers. This was codenamed Operation Hardboiled and consisted of a notional assault on the Norwegian mainland. Armed forces were appointed for this operation and training began for landings near Stavanger (although these amphibious forces were eventually employed in operations against Vichy-held Madagascar in May 1942).

A Focke-Wulf Fw200C-3 on a French airfield, probably Bordeaux-Mérignac or Cognac, being refuelled from a petrol bowser on the left and a wagon with a pump-handle on the right.

Jean-Louis Roba collection

Norwegian interpreters were appointed, supplies of Norwegian currency were provided and rumours of the impending operation were deliberately leaked in London. These rumours found their way to Stockholm by January 1942 and were evidently believed, for strong reinforcements of German garrisons in Norway began soon afterwards, drawing men away from the true areas of conflict.

In addition, Hitler recalled his major battle units, the *Scharnhorst*, *Gneisenau* and *Prinz Eugen*, from Brest to German waters. From there they could join the newly commissioned battleship *Tirpitz*, sister-ship of the *Bismarck*, which sailed from Kiel and reached Trondheim on

16 January 1942. This contingency had been long anticipated by the British and plans to destroy the warships en route through the Channel had been drawn up as early as 29 April 1941. Three other possibilities had been considered at the time. These were that the warships might try to break out into the Atlantic, or into the Mediterranean, or return to Germany around the north of the British Isles. However, the first was dismissed as unlikely since refuelling facilities were not available. The second seemed improbable since the Royal Navy's powerful Force H at Gibraltar stood in their way, while the third was equally unlikely since they would encounter the Home Fleet at Scapa Flow in the Orkneys. It seemed almost certain that the three enemy warships would attempt to make a run through the Straits of Dover, screened by destroyers, torpedo-boats, minesweepers and E-boats. They would be under the umbrella of the Luftwaffe and would avoid the British heavy warships.

The Admiralty and the RAF had made detailed plans to counter this probability, under the codename Operation Fuller. They instituted a system of air patrols around Brest, dispatched two submarines to those waters, and allocated torpedo-bombers and other strike aircraft of Coastal Command and Fleet Air Arm to the operation, as well as various squadrons of Fighter Command and Bomber Command. The Royal Navy laid numerous mines and allocated destroyers and motor torpedo-boats to intercept the enemy battle fleet. Bomber Command also laid mines off the Frisian Islands.

A state of alert was ordered on 3 February 1942 by both the Admiralty and the RAF when Enigma decrypts established that the officer commanding battleships, Vizeadmiral Otto Ciliax, had hoisted his flag in the *Scharnhorst* and that the warships were carrying out exercises. The precise date of sailing was not known, but on 8 and 9 February RAF photo-reconnaissance verified that the warships were still in dock.

On the German side the fighter ace Oberst (Group Captain) Adolf Galland had been summoned on 12 January 1942 to a conference with naval and air leaders in Hitler's 'Wolf Lair' to plan the break-out, and was appointed by Goering to handle the air cover. The operation was codenamed 'Cerberus' by the Kriegs-marine but Galland chose 'Donnerkeil' (Thunderbolt) for the Luftwaffe. The Germans decided later to leave Brest on the night of 11/12 February, when a depression from Iceland was expected to reach the Channel, bringing low cloud and reducing visibility.

A night raid on Brest by eighteen Wellingtons of Bomber Command delayed the start by a couple of hours until 22.45 hours, but the passage of the German fleet around the Armorican peninsula and through the Channel coincided with a series of mishaps on the British side and created a situation which was later described as a fiasco. When the German fleet rounded the island of Ushant at about midnight, the submarine on patrol, HMS *Sealion*, happened to be about 30 miles away, recharging its batteries. ASV radar in the patrolling Hudson of Coastal Command developed trouble and the crew returned to base for repair. They took off again and once more the ASV failed. Exactly the same happened with another Hudson sent to relieve the first machine.

By dawn on 12 February the first of the escorting Messerschmitt Bf110 night-fighters arrived over the German warships, which steamed up the Channel at about 28 knots, while the British remained unaware of their presence. About 80 minesweepers preceded the warships, clearing a channel ahead. Galland had produced a masterpiece of planning. About 250 of his fighter aircraft, Bf110s, Bf109s and Fw190s, hopped from airfield to airfield eastwards along the north coast of France, providing continuous air cover. Morale among the German pilots and crews was extremely high, with any thought of fatigue dismissed by the realisation that they were contributing to a remarkable tactical success.

After 08.30 hours the RAF's ground radar stations began to notice intermittent plots of enemy aircraft circling over small areas. The Germans had been gradually intensifying interference with these stations during the previous few days, and at this stage the British operators did not pick up the movement of the enemy battle fleet. These began to appear on the screens at Beachy Head at 10.00 hours. Two Spitfires were sent up for reconnaissance at 10.20 hours and the pilots spotted the enemy vessels, which by then had reached a position about 15 miles west of Le Touquet. The Spitfires landed 30 minutes after take-off and at last the British knew that a major operation was under way, but it was too late to arrange a coordinated attack.

Soon afterwards the German battle fleet came under fire from the coastal batteries at Dover. The gun crews fired their 9.2-inch guns but their shells missed the targets by wide margins. Five little motor torpedo-boats which put out from Dover had difficulty penetrating the German destroyer and E-boat screen and their torpedoes were fired from too long a range. Six torpedo-carrying Fairey Swordfish of the Fleet Air Arm's 825 Squadron took off from Manston at 12.25 hours and set course for the target north of Calais, led by Lieutenant-Commander Eugene Esmonde and escorted by ten Spitfires. Their heroic attack was suicidal. The Spitfires became separated from their slow-flying charges in the overcast weather and all six Swordfish were shot down by enemy fighters or the wall of flak. Esmonde was awarded a posthumous Victoria Cross.

Next in the series of ill-coordinated attacks were the Beauforts, which were scattered around the country, at Thorney Island in Sussex, St Eval in Cornwall and Leuchars in Fife. The first to attack were five Beauforts of 217 Squadron from Thorney Island (where the author was Squadron Duty Officer for the day). These took off in two flights at slightly different times but did not make contact with their fighter escorts and all were attacked by enemy fighters off the Hook of Holland. One was shot down and the other four dropped their torpedoes from very long range at about 15.40 hours at a battleship which appeared to be stationary, but scored no hits.

Shortly before this attack, at 15.31 hours, the *Scharnhorst* had struck a magnetic mine dropped by Bomber Command. She came to a halt, with the leading destroyer *Z29* in attendance, while the rest of the naval formation continued at speed. Both stationary German vessels came under attack from bomber aircraft at this stage but the weather was deteriorating rapidly. The nearest bombs fell about 100 yards to port while the Luftwaffe fighter escorts engaged the RAF bombers.

At 16.05 hours the *Scharnhorst* got under way again, moving slowly but having suffered less damage than originally feared. Seven Beauforts of 42 Squadron, which had flown down from Leuchars to Manston in Kent, attacked the *Gneisenau* and the *Prinz Eugen* at about 16.05 hours, but there were no hits. Five Hudsons accompanied them but their bombs missed. These two enemy warships were also engaged at 16.45 hours by five destroyers from the 16th and 21st Flotillas from Harwich, which fired salvoes of torpedoes from ranges of about 3,000 yards while under heavy gunfire. All the torpedoes missed. The destroyer HMS *Worcester* was badly hit by gunfire but managed to return to Harwich under her own steam. Two more Beauforts of 217 Squadron from Thorney Island made attacks off Ijmuiden, at 17.10 hours and 18.00 hours

The battleships *Scharnhorst* and *Gneisenau* steaming up mid-Channel during their escape from Brest on 12 February 1942. The photograph was taken from the heavy cruiser *Prinz Eugen*.

Author's collection

respectively, without result. Twelve Beauforts of 86 and 217 Squadrons, which had flown across from St Eval to Coltishall in Norfolk, took off at 17.01 hours but failed to find the enemy fleet in darkness and low cloud. Two of these aircraft failed to return.

Apart from these attacks by Coastal Command, 242 aircraft were dispatched by Bomber Command in three waves, between 14.30 and 18.10 hours. They were intended to bomb the ships from medium level but most were thwarted by low cloud, poor visibility and enemy fighters. Only 39 were able to bomb, in extremely difficult conditions, and none scored hits. Fifteen failed to return and many others were damaged. Fighter Command dispatched 398 aircraft, some of which strafed the smaller escort vessels and scored hits, while others were engaged in combat with enemy aircraft. Seventeen of these RAF fighters were lost.

The Luftwaffe suffered minimal losses. Three Fw190s and one BF109 failed to return, as well as three Dornier Do17s sent out on reconnaissance. Several other aircraft were damaged in combat but managed to return to their airfields. Vizeadmiral Ciliax had good reason to breathe a sigh of relief as his vessels neared their home ports in complete darkness, and to congratulate himself on achieving a splendid victory. But his troubles were not yet over. At 19.55 hours, when off the island of Terschelling, the *Gneisenau* hit another of the magnetic mines dropped by the RAF. She was able to get under way again and eventually anchored with the *Prinz Eugen* off the mouth of the Elbe for the night. At 21.34

hours the slower-moving *Scharnhorst* struck yet another magnetic mine in the same area, and this time was far more seriously damaged. She limped along at 10 knots, arriving at Wilhelmshaven the following morning to begin undergoing extensive repairs.

During daylight on 13 February the *Gneisenau* and *Prinz Eugen* passed through the Kaiser Wilhelm Canal to Kiel, where repairs on the former began. But both were to suffer further damage. Off Trondheim ten days later the *Prinz Eugen* was struck in the stern by a torpedo fired by the submarine HMS *Trident*. She managed to reach Trondheim but took little part in the remainder of the war. The *Gneisenau* suffered an even worse fate. Her bows were hit by a bomb dropped during a raid by Bomber Command against Kiel on the night of 26/27 February 1942, which killed 116 of her crew. Her guns were removed pending replacement and the shattered vessel was taken to Gdynia for repair and conversion, but the plan to adapt her was eventually abandoned.

German propaganda rejoiced in the success of the German battle fleet in passing through the Channel, but made no mention of the subsequent damage to the warships. Their high commanders were more realistic, commenting privately that it was a tactical success but a strategic defeat. The misfortunes suffered by the enemy warships were known to the British high commanders through Enigma decrypts at Bletchley Park, but such close secrets could never be passed to the public. The British press railed against the national humiliation and the inefficiency of the armed services, with some justification in respect of the failure of coordination. But at least the threat that German surface warships posed to Britain's lifeline across the Atlantic had been removed. This would be fought henceforth by Allied warships and aircraft against U-boats and Italian submarines. If those British journalists had but known it, far more serious events were already unfolding in the western part of that turbulent ocean.

Air Chief Marshal Sir Philip B. Joubert de la Ferté, the Air Officer Commanding-in-Chief of Coastal Command from 14 June 1941 to 4 February 1943.

Author's collection

The battleship HMS *Duke of York* in an Icelandic fjord, with a destroyer moored off her starboard bow and snow-capped mountains in the distance.

Author's collection

Two Sea Hurricane IAs of the RAF being ferried on a barge to a Catapult Aircraft Merchantman, known as a CAM-ship. The letters LU on the nearer Hurricane are those of the Merchant Ship Fighter Unit (MSFU). Most of the pilots were volunteers from the RAF, trained on catapult take-offs. This training took place from January 1942 at the Royal Aircraft Establishment at Farnborough and from July 1941 at RAF Speke in Lancashire.

Author's collection

A Sea Hurricane IA of the RAF's Merchant Ship Fighter Unit, serial V6756, perched on the catapult of the CAM-ship *Empire Tide*. These vessels were adapted from freighters and crewed by merchant seamen under the Red Ensign. The main purpose of the Hurricanes was to tackle long-range bombers such as Focke-Wulf Fw200 Condors based at Mérignac near Bordeaux, which were harrying vessels in convoys.

Author's collection

A Sea Hurricane IA on a Catapult Aircraft Merchantman, ready for take-off. The catapult was angled across the ship, partly to prevent the blast of the rocket from damaging the bridge of the vessel, and partly to reduce the possibility of the vessel colliding with the Hurricane if something went wrong and it plunged into the sea. The Hurricane was regarded as expendable. After any combat, the pilot had to ditch or bale out in the hope of being picked up, or fly to land within range.

Author's collection

A Sea Hurricane IB of the Fleet Air Arm landing on the training carrier HMS *Argus*. The early machines were converted from Hurricane IBs, being fitted with arrester hooks. This type of machine became widely known as 'an 'Urricane with an 'ook', after a remark by a puzzled Cockney ground mechanic when he saw one for the first time.

Author's collection

Escort vessels of an Atlantic convoy, burdened with snow and ice, seen through the davits of a Canadian minesweeper, also covered with ice. Type 272 radars are visible on the ships' bridges.

Author's collection

The 28-cm guns of the German pocket battleship *Deutschland* opening fire. This heavy cruiser of 11,700 tons was renamed *Lützow* in November 1939 since Hitler believed that a warship carrying the original name should not be exposed to the danger of sinking.

Author's collection

The crew of Beaufort I serial L9939 of 42 Squadron, which crippled the cruiser *Lützow* on 13 June 1941. The letter of their aircraft was W, and they called it 'Wreck'. Left to right: Flight Sergeant L. Ray Loveitt (pilot); Sergeant Percy Wallace-Pannell, seated (turret gunner); Sergeant Al Morris, Canadian (navigator); Sergeant Downing (wireless operator).

Ralph Barker via Roger Hayward

Catalina I serial AJ519 of 413 (RCAF) Squadron, being bombed up at Gibraltar. The squadron operated over the North Atlantic from October 1941 but in March 1942 began moving to Ceylon.

Author's collection

A Consolidated Catalina practising with smoke-bombs.

Author's collection

An air gunner in a Consolidated Catalina of Coastal Command on lookout duty beside the blister fitted with twin Vickers 0.303-inch machine-guns.

Author's collection

Fitting Mark VA depth-charges of 450 lb from an explosives barge to the racks under the wings of a Consolidated Catalina at RAF Oban in Argyllshire.

Bruce Robertson collection

A Lockheed Hudson Mark III of 269 Squadron on the bleak airfield at Wick in Caithness, where the squadron was based from 10 October 1939 to 11 April 1941. Note the roller in the foreground, partly sunk in the mud. The Hudson was the first American aircraft employed by RAF squadrons in the Second World War, having entered service in May 1939. The Mark III was powered by two Wright Cyclone engines of 1,200hp and had a respectable endurance of about six hours. It was armed with two machine-guns firing forward, two in the dorsal turret, two firing in beam positions and one in a ventral position (shown here extended). It could carry four 250lb depth-charges.

Wing Commander John C. Graham DFC

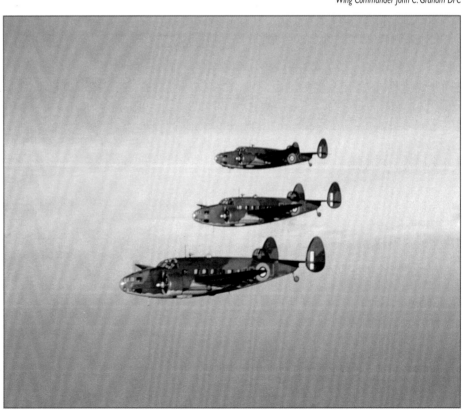

Hudson IIIs from No. 6 Operational Training Unit at Thornaby in Yorkshire, photographed on 15 December 1941.

RAF Museum P100465

A Hudson of 269 Squadron taking off from Kaldarnes in Iceland, probably in a dim early morning light. The squadron operated from this airfield from 12 April 1941 to 6 May 1943, engaged on convoy protection duties and hunting for U-boats. It forced the surrender of *U-570*, sank three other U-boats and damaged three more.

Wing Commander John C. Graham DFC*

Winston Churchill in the pilot's seat of the Boeing 314A flying boat *Berwick* of the British Overseas Airways Corporation, en route from Washington to Bermuda on 14 January 1942 under the captaincy of Commander Kelly Rogers. Churchill had arrived in Washington on 22 December in the battleship HMS *Duke of York*, to discuss joint strategy following the entry of the USA into the war. On arrival in Bermuda he decided to return to England in this flying boat, rather than in HMS *Duke of York* with the remainder of his party. Boeing 314As were employed by both BOAC and Pan American Airways on regular North Atlantic crossings. The flight on the following day lasted over twenty hours. For much of the time the aircraft was in thick cloud, leading to the alarming discovery that they were heading towards Brest. A change of course brought the flying boat to a safe touch-down at Plymouth.

Author's collection

Blindfolded German survivors of U-boats sunk by British forces while disembarking at a port, en route to an interrogation centre and eventually a prisoner-of-war camp.

Author's collection

Flower class corvettes of the Royal Canadian Navy. Canada built over 150 of these warships, which began coming into service in early 1941. Many of the crewmen were inexperienced volunteers but they soon made up for any shortcomings with their determination.

Author's collection

The Flower class corvette HMS *Cyclamen*, of 1,170 tons displacement, photographed in 1942. Fitted with a steam engine of 2,750hp, these escorts were lively but could achieve a maximum speed of only 16.5 knots. The armament included a 4-inch gun forward, a 2-pounder pom-pom and lighter machine-guns aft, plus depth-charges. The anti-submarine suite included a Type 272 radar in its characteristic 'lantern' ahead of the funnel. The *Cyclamen* was one of several to incorporate a number of improvements over earlier ships of this class. Most significant was a lengthened forecastle to improve seakeeping and dryness, as in the later 'Modified' corvettes.

Maritime Photo Library

Sunderland II serial W3989 of 228 Squadron. This mark was introduced at the end of 1941, powered by four Bristol Pegasus XVIII engines of 1,065hp. Mark II air-to-surface vessel radar was fitted to these Sunderlands.

Author's collection

Mark XI 250lb depth-charges on bomb carriage rails inside a Sunderland Mark V. The rails were run out from the sides of the fuselage before the depth-charges were dropped.

Roger Hayward collection

Following the decision to deny the coal reserves of the Norwegian island of Spitsbergen to the Germans, the Royal Navy mounted an expedition in late August 1941. The cruisers *Nigeria* and *Aurora* sailed from Scapa Flow, together with several destroyers. They escorted the liner *Empress of Canada*, carrying about 650 troops, mostly Canadians but with some Norwegians and a few British sappers. This photograph shows the troops embarking for the shore in Advent Bay, Spitsbergen.

Author's collection

(*Opposite, top*) The troops removed or destroyed vital equipment at the coal mines in Spitsbergen. The coal dumps were set on fire. Almost all the Norwegian miners, as well as some Russian settlers, were rounded up and taken to Britain, as shown here. The operation was completed on 3 September 1941.

Author's collection

(*Opposite, bottom*) Installations left on fire at Advent Bay in Spitsbergen after the raiding party left on 3 September 1941.

Author's collection

The first British combined operation of the war took place on 27 December 1941 when a cruiser and four destroyers of the Royal Navy carried Commandos to the islands of Vaasgö and Maalöy near Bergen in Norway. Bomber Command provided 19 Blenheims and 10 Hampdens to support the operation. Of these, 13 Blenheim IVs of 114 Squadron made a low-level attack on the nearby fighter airfield of Herdla. This F24 mirror photograph shows a Messerschmitt Bf109 taking off, while behind is an Arado Ar96B training monoplane. Below the Bf109 is a Focke-Wulf Fw58 utility aircraft.

Author's collection

(*Opposite, top*) Bombs exploding on Herdla airfield and flak bursts in the water. Two Blenheims collided and the six crew members were killed. There were numerous craters left in the airfield and a workshop was destroyed. Two Germans were killed and three wounded.

Author's collection

(*Opposite, bottom*) British Commandos attacking the German garrison at Maalöy, under cover of a smokescreen. Norwegian troops also took part in the operation. The German garrisons on the two islands were overcome, with twenty-five men killed and many others captured. The attackers suffered only light casualties. They destroyed five merchant ships totalling 16,650 tons, blew up munitions dumps and storehouses, set fire to oil tanks and destroyed a radio station. They also brought back many Norwegian volunteers to join the British forces.

Author's collection

A firing party at the military funeral of German sailors killed during one of the RAF's raids on Brest.

Part of the German escort during the 'Channel Dash' of 12 February 1942 – a destroyer, a torpedo-boat and Messerschmitt Bf110s.

The heavy cruiser *Prinz Eugen* firing her anti-aircraft guns in action during the 'Channel Dash' of 12 February 1942.

Author's collection

A Handley Page Hampden fitted by the Royal Aircraft Establishment with a carrier and a dummy A1 Mark I mine of nominally 1,500lb. Magnetic sea mines dropped by Coastal Command off the shores of France, Belgium and Holland resulted in many sinkings of German vessels, as did those dropped by Bomber Command off the coasts of Denmark, Germany and in the Baltic. Other surface vessels were damaged, causing much disruption to enemy coastal traffic. It is probable that some of the U-boats that were lost for unknown reasons fell victim to these mines.

Roger Hayward collection

The Channel Dash by Charles J. Thompson GAvA, ASAA, GMA, EAA

Fairey Swordfish II serial W5984 of the Fleet Air Arm's 825 Squadron, flown by Lieutenant-Commander Eugene Esmonde DSO, under attack on 12 February 1942 by a Focke-Wulf Fw190A-1 of 9./Jagdgeschwader 2. Although his aircraft was shredded by cannon fire, Esmonde led his six Swordfish in a torpedo attack against the German battle fleet. All the Swordfish were destroyed. Esmonde was awarded a posthumous Victoria Cross.

Oberleutnant Johannes Naumann (right) explains with the aid of a painting how he shot down two Fairey Swordfish in his Focke-Wulf Fw190A-1 of 9./Jagdgeschwader 26 on 12 February 1942.

A. Richard Chapman collection

This Messerschmitt Bf109E-7 of 7./Jagdgeschwader 1 took off from Brest on 12 February 1942 to form part of the escort for the German battle fleet but suffered engine trouble when over the Channel. The pilot, Feldwebel Heinz Beyer, headed for Octeville airfield, near Cherbourg, but the engine cut out and he made a forced landing. The machine tipped over and Beyer hung upside down for a quarter of an hour before being pulled clear by French civilians, having suffered nothing worse than shock, various bruises and a broken nose. He did not require hospital treatment and the Messerschmitt was rated as 50 per cent damaged.

Jean-Louis Roba collection

A Mark VIII torpedo being loaded on a Fairey
Swordfish by RAF men, probably photographed at a
time when marine aviation was in the hands of the
Fleet Air Arm of the RAF.

Author's collection

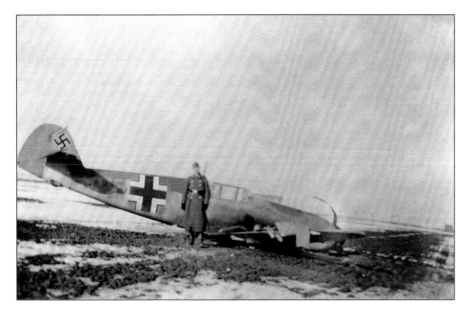

A Messerschmitt Bf109F-4 of II./Jagdgeschwader 2, photographed in the Low Countries on 12 February 1942. It is probably works number 9562, which damaged its undercarriage when landing at Vlissengen airfield on returning from the Channel Dash operation.

Gerrit J. Zwanenburg collection

The well-known German fighter ace Egon Mayer, Staffelkapitän of 7./Jagdgeschwader 2, who flew during the Channel Dash. By 5 February 1944 he had been credited with 100 victories on the 'Channel Front'. He was killed in combat with USAAF P-47 Thunderbolts on 2 February 1944, while leading one of his groups, and was buried in the cemetery at Beaumont-le-Roger, south-west of Rouen.

Jean-Louis Roba collection

A pilot of I./Jagdgeschwader 26 returning from an operation in his Messerschmitt Bf109F-4.

Jean-Louis Roba collection

Messerschmitt Bf110E-1s of II./Nachtjagdgeschwader 1, which took part in the last phase of the Channel Dash when stationed at Koksijde in Belgium. This photograph was taken at a different location.

Author's collection

Some of the aircrews of II./Nachtjagdgeschwader 1, which took part in the last phase of the Channel Dash.

Author's collection

The heavy cruiser *Prinz Eugen*, of 14,800 tons displacement, escaped unscathed during the Channel Dash of 11–12 February 1942 but was struck by a torpedo fired by the submarine HMS *Trident* off Trondheim on 23 February 1942. This caused severe damage to her stern. After undergoing temporary repairs in Norway, during which she was fitted with a jury stern, she sailed to Kiel for permanent repairs, as shown here. While en route, she escaped damage from an attack by a large force of Beauforts and Hudsons of Coastal Command on 17 May 1942. She was finally destroyed by the Americans during their post-war atomic bomb tests in the Pacific.

Jean-Louis Roba collection

A close-up of the German battleship *Tirpitz*, of 42,900 tons displacement, taken on 28 March 1942 at Aasfjord near Trondheim by a Spitfire of No. 1 Photographic Reconnaissance Unit flown from Wick in Caithness by Flight Lieutenant Alfred F.P. Fane.

Author's collection

CHAPTER FOUR

HAVOC IN THE ATLANTIC

Germany's declaration of war against the USA on 11 December 1941
had given Admiral Karl Dönitz an unparalleled opportunity in the
Western Atlantic, but he was unable to take full advantage of this for
several weeks, since he had to obey Hitler's orders. His preferred
target area was the eastern seaboard of America, from the Caribbean to the states
of New England, along which sailed the densest mercantile traffic in the world,
carrying cargoes such as oil, cotton, sugar and various minerals. According to his
diary, he had 91 operational U-boats on 1 January 1942, but of these 23 were in
the Mediterranean. Another 6 were deployed on the approaches to Gibraltar,
while 4 more were off the Norwegian coasts. Of the remaining 58, 36 were
undergoing maintenance and repairs, delayed by shortages of suitable labour.
This left only 22 U-boats available for the North Atlantic, and of these half were
always en route to, or returning from, their distant operational area.

Thus there were 11 U-boats in positions to attack shipping in the Atlantic, and
of these only 5 began operations off the east coast of America, after setting out to
the area at the end of December 1941. Yet this handful began to wreak havoc in
their new waters. They found conditions which were quite extraordinary. No
preparations for anti-submarine warfare seemed to have been made. The
merchant vessels were sailing independently and without protection, either from
deck armament or from naval escorts. There was no blackout along the shores
and the German navigation officers were able to pinpoint their positions
precisely. Operating separately, the U-boats were able to submerge along the
shipping lanes during darkness and then surface in daylight to pick off their
victims with impunity, like wolves among flocks of sheep. They even sank ships
by gunfire on some occasions, rather than expend their limited supplies of
torpedoes. This was the beginning of the period called the 'Second Happy Time'
by German submariners.

Sinking and burning ships littered these waters. In January 1942 some 48
merchant ships totalling about 277,000 tons were sunk off the American
seaboard and in the North Atlantic. The first five U-boats were joined by three
more towards the end of January. Only three U-boats were sunk in that month,
all by the British in mid-Atlantic.

On 1 February a serious setback occurred at Bletchley Park when the U-boats
in the Atlantic introduced a fourth rotor into their Enigma machines and their

messages could no longer be decrypted. These signals were designated 'Triton' by the Germans and 'Shark' by Bletchley Park. The cipher used by U-boat crews under training in the Baltic, named 'Thetis', was unchanged, as was the 'Hydra' cipher employed for Home Waters. The cryptanalysts were able to continue identifying U-boat movements in and out of Norwegian and French ports, but not in the North Atlantic.

Sinkings in February rose to 73 ships totalling about 430,000 tons in the North Atlantic, including 31 off the American coasts. British warships sank only two U-boats in the North Atlantic. By then, Dönitz had decided to move his other U-boats to the west, increasing the proportion of sinkings off the American coasts. The U-boats also entered the Gulf of Mexico, which proved another profitable hunting ground. The ten Italian long-distance submarines of Betasom, based at Bordeaux ('Beta' for the initial of the city and 'som' for 'sommergibili', or submarines), shared in the numerous victories in these waters, without loss.

With regard to American aircraft, the US Army controlled most land-based aircraft while the US Navy controlled seaplanes and floatplanes, plus carrier-borne aircraft. Blimps were also employed by the US Navy for reconnaissance purposes, supplementing the few aircraft available for the vast areas that needed to be covered. For example, during January 1942 the enormous Eastern Sea Frontier of America was swept each day by only two land-based aircraft. It was not until 1 March 1942 that the Americans succeeded in sinking a U-boat, when a Hudson of Squadron VP-82 of the US Navy successfully attacked the Type VIIC *U-656* off the coast of Newfoundland. The same squadron sank the Type VIIC *U-503* in the same area on 15 March 1942, but no U-boats were sunk off the coasts of the USA. Sinkings of merchant ships rose to higher levels in March: 95 ships, totalling about 534,000 tons, were sunk in the North Atlantic, and

The Type IXB *U-109*, commanded by Kapitänleutnant Heinrich Bleichrodt, operated off the coast of Florida in the spring of 1942. This was one of the long-range U-boats, built with a wide upper deck and equipped with a 105-mm gun. It was sunk about 800 miles west of Land's End on 4 May 1943, when commanded by Oberleutnant zur See Joachim Schramm, by Liberator V serial FL955 of 86 Squadron, flown on convoy escort duties from Aldergrove in Northern Ireland by Pilot Officer J.C. Green. Four depth-charges were dropped after the initial sighting and wreckage came to the surface, surrounded by a huge patch of oil. There were no survivors. The U-boat was on its ninth war cruise and had sunk thirteen Allied vessels.

Jak P. Mallmann Showell collection

another 3, totalling 15,000 tons, in the South Atlantic. The British sank three U-boats in the North Atlantic during March. Another was lost, apparently after striking a German mine.

The reason for this massacre of American ships is not hard to find. It was the policy of the US Navy, under Admiral Ernest J. King, to send its anti-submarine warships out on offensive patrols rather than employ them on convoy protection. The convoy system, the benefits of which had become glaringly apparent from the experiences of both the First and Second World Wars, were not adopted for about six months. Of course, the resources of the US Navy were stretched to an almost impossible degree by the war in the Pacific, although 'Germany first' had become the agreed Anglo-American policy during Churchill's visit to Washington in January 1942. However, other forces came under the control of the US Navy, such as the cutters of the US Coastguard and armed trawlers, as well as some converted yachts. In addition, submarine-chasers were being built, although these were not wholly suitable for the rigours of the Atlantic Ocean. But no convoys

A tanker engulfed in flames off the coast of Florida, after an attack by a U-boat.

Author's collection

were formed for them to protect, and all were engaged on roving patrols. Instead, the Americans tried routing the merchant ships closer to shore and gathering them at night in protected anchorages, so that they sailed only on short runs during daylight. But these measures availed nothing and the losses continued.

On 8 February 1942 the coastal defences off North America were divided into the Canadian Coastal Zone, the Eastern Sea Frontier, the Caribbean Sea Frontier and the Gulf Sea Frontier. US warships patrolled these waters for four months from the entry of their country into the war, without sinking a single U-boat. It was not until 14 April that they scored their first victory, when the destroyer USS *Roper* sank the Type VIIB *U-85* off Cape Hatteras in North Carolina.

In April 1942 66 merchant ships totalling about 391,000 tons were sunk in the North Atlantic, many of them in American waters. Another 8 were sunk in the South Atlantic, totalling about 48,000 tons. The British sank only one U-boat in April, while another was lost from unknown causes. The effect of the U-boats became even more deadly at the end of that month, when they began to receive supplies from the first of the Type XIV 'Milch-cow' U-boats. These brought fuel, torpedoes, spare parts and food across the Atlantic, enabling the operational U-boats to extend the periods of their war cruises. Meanwhile, Admiral King decided that the implementation of a convoy system in home waters would have to wait until more escorts became available.

The concentration of U-boats off America gave some relief to the Royal Navy and the RAF's Coastal Command, both of which were receiving increased resources. In January 1942 the Royal Navy's Western Approaches Command had available for the North Atlantic about 70 destroyers, 18 sloops and 67 corvettes, together with 10 cutters transferred from the US Coastguard. In addition, destroyers of the US Navy escorted some convoys, principally those bringing American supplies across the Atlantic.

The strength of Coastal Command had also increased. In January 1942 there were 23 Sunderlands available for Atlantic waters, as well as 19 Wellingtons and 37 Whitleys. There were numerous Hudsons, although not all these were employed in the North Atlantic; those engaged in anti-submarine warfare operated mainly from Iceland and Northern Ireland. There were four Beaufort squadrons, although in the next few months these would be sent to the Middle East to help in operations against Axis convoys. For the VLR (very long range) force, there were 38 Catalinas but only 10 of the precious and much-needed Liberators. However, more of these VLR aircraft were being produced. The Fleet Air Arm had also grown considerably from its total of 232 aircraft at the beginning of the war. Figures for April 1942 show that it had a strength of 446 aircraft – 175 fighters, 196 torpedo-bombers and 75 reconnaissance aircraft.

The potential menace of the new battleship *Tirpitz* in her Norwegian fjord continued to worry the Admiralty. It was considered that she might break out into the Atlantic, following the wake of the *Bismarck*, and play havoc with a convoy before making for shelter in a French port. Although there was no indication of any such German plan, it was known that there was only one port in western France which was large enough for her to berth. This was the great lock in St Nazaire at the mouth of the River Loire, which had been built to accommodate the liner *Normandie* and was also available as a dry dock. Accordingly, the destruction of this lock was planned, and an attack took place on the night of 27/28 March 1942.

It was a combined operation. Some 35 Whitleys and 27 Wellingtons of Bomber Command were dispatched to bomb the port as a diversionary measure, although low cloud prevented most from identifying the target. Flying German colours on her approach and making false identity signals as *ruses de guerre*, the ex-American destroyer HMS *Campbeltown*, loaded with 3 tons of explosives, was rammed against the outer caisson of the lock, while motor launches landed naval forces and Commandos under intense fire. The men stormed ashore and began the work of destruction, before the *Campbeltown* blew up and destroyed the lock gates. Sadly, 85 men of the Royal Navy and 59 of the Army were killed, while many others were taken prisoner. Anticipating more attacks of this nature, Hitler ordered the U-boat headquarters in Lorient to be moved inland, and they were transferred to Paris. In spite of the casualties, this attack was rated as a brilliant success, in the best traditions of the British armed services. It was many months before the lock gates would be rebuilt, and the *Tirpitz* never entered the Atlantic.

The unhappy state of affairs along the American seaboard continued. In May 1942 120 ships totalling about 576,000 tons were sunk in the North Atlantic, including the coastal waters of the USA. Another 2 were sunk in the South Atlantic, totalling about 9,000 tons. By this time, there were 12 U-boats operating off the east coast of America, with 20 more in the Caribbean or the Gulf of Mexico. Only one of these U-boats was sunk, the Type *U-352* by the coastguard cutter USS *Icarus* on 9 May. British warships and the RAF sank three other U-boats elsewhere in the North Atlantic during this month.

June 1942 was even worse, with 124 vessels totalling 623,000 tons sunk in the North Atlantic, plus 4 more totalling about 26,000 tons in the South Atlantic.

Only three U-boats were lost, 2 to US warships and aircraft and one to a combination of Coastal Command and the Fleet Air Arm. It seemed that Germany was winning the Battle of the Atlantic. But then the Americans suddenly adopted the tried and tested convoy system. From the end of June sinkings in their waters dropped dramatically. Dönitz immediately recognised the changed situation and moved many of his U-boats to the mid-Atlantic, where they could attack the convoys outside the range of most shore-based aircraft but where the battle would be much harder to fight. The 'Second Happy Time' for German submariners had come to an end. The Italian submarines continued to hunt in the more southerly latitudes of the Atlantic, as did some of the long-distance U-boats.

In June 1942 a strange new device appeared in the night skies over the Bay of Biscay. This was the 'Leigh Light', a powerful airborne searchlight named after its inventor Squadron Leader Humphrey de Verde 'Sammy' Leigh. It was carried in a Wellington VIII specially adapted for this purpose. The light had been tested and the tactics perfected by the Coastal Command Development Unit. No. 172 Squadron, formed on 4 April 1942 at Chivenor in North Devon, was the first to be equipped with these new machines. They were also fitted with ASV Mark II radar and after a period of training the crews were ready to operate over the Bay of Biscay. It was known that U-boats travelled on the surface over the Bay at night, to charge their batteries, and then submerged near convoys to seek their victims.

Four of these Wellingtons took off from Chivenor in the late evening of 3 June 1942 for their first operation, each covering a different area. Three found nothing and turned back at the end of their patrols. The fourth, Wellington serial

The Type VIIC *U-71*, commanded by Kapitänleutnant Walter Flachsenberg, was damaged in the afternoon of 5 June 1942 when outward bound from La Pallice in France. It was surprised on the surface by Short Sunderland serial W3986 of 10 (RAAF) Squadron, flown from Mount Batten by Flight Lieutenant S.R.C. Wood, which dropped eight depth-charges and made machine-gun attacks. The U-boat dived but was damaged and forced to return to La Pallice. The Sunderland was then engaged in an air battle with a Focke-Wulf Fw200 Condor, in which both aircraft were damaged but able to return to their bases.

Author's collection

ES986 flown by Squadron Leader Jeaffreson H. Greswell, picked up a radar trace shortly after 02.00 hours on the following morning, near the north coast of Spain. He dived and switched on the Leigh Light, but at first overshot the target. Estimating that he had been slightly too high, he tried again and the submarine showed up squarely in the beam. To his amazement he was greeted only by coloured flares, but he dropped a stick of four depth-charges which straddled the target.

Unknown to him, this was a large Italian submarine, the *Luigi Torelli*, under the command of Tenente di Vascello (Lieutenant) Count Augusto Migliorini, which had left La Pallice in the afternoon of 2 June for its seventh war cruise in the area of the West Indies. Having no depth-charges left, Greswell turned for home but came across another submarine, which he also illuminated. This was the Italian *Morosini*, under the command of Tenente di Vascello Francesco d'Allessandreo, which had left La Pallice at the same time as the *Luigi Torrelli*, but this time the Wellington could attack only with machine-gun fire.

It is now known that the men of the *Luigi Torelli* were puzzled by the searchlight beam; thinking it must have been from a German aircraft, they fired recognition signals. Their boat was badly damaged, brought to a halt and set on fire near the forward batteries, but the experienced crew managed to put out the fire and get the engines going. It limped to the coast and was beached for emergency repairs. Towed off by Spanish tugs during the next evening, it was reberthed near the port of Aviles.

It set off again on the evening of 6 June, heading back to Bordeaux and unable to dive, but was attacked the next day by two Sunderlands of 10 (RAAF) Squadron. Badly damaged, it managed to reach Santander and eventually headed for Bordeaux on 14 July, arriving the following day. The other submarine, *Morosini*, continued its war cruise in the Caribbean but was lost from unknown causes after sending its last signal on 8 August when approaching the French coast.

The first destruction of a U-boat by a Leigh Light Wellington took place in the early morning of 6 July 1942, when the Type IXC *U-502*, commanded by Kapitänleutnant Jürgen von Rosenstiel, was sunk with all hands when returning to Lorient by a Wellington VIII of 172 Squadron flown by an American in the RAF, Pilot Officer Wiley B. Howell. These aircraft had become a major thorn in the flesh of the U-boat commanders travelling through the Bay of Biscay. So many attacks were made at night with the Leigh Light that on 16 July Dönitz ordered a reversal of their previous procedure. Henceforth they were to sail on the surface during daylight hours, even though this exposed them to attacks by the anti-submarine aircraft operating at these times.

Wellingtons, Whitleys and Sunderlands of Coastal Command intensified their patrols over the Bay in daylight, searching for these U-boats on the surface. Of course, these increased activities worried the Germans, who required a long-range fighter to combat the RAF aircraft. The answer was found with a version of the Junkers Ju88, a variant known as the C-6 'Zerstörer' (Destroyer), with which V Gruppe of Kampfgeschwader 40 began to be equipped at the end of June 1942. These new Ju88C-6s were based at Lorient, Vannes and Bordeaux-Mérignac. Fitted with increased armament, their main task was to attack the RAF aircraft threatening the safe passage of U-boats over these waters. Many combats took place, beginning with the destruction of a Wellington of 311 (Czech) Squadron on 15 July 1942. However, the Luftwaffe did not have

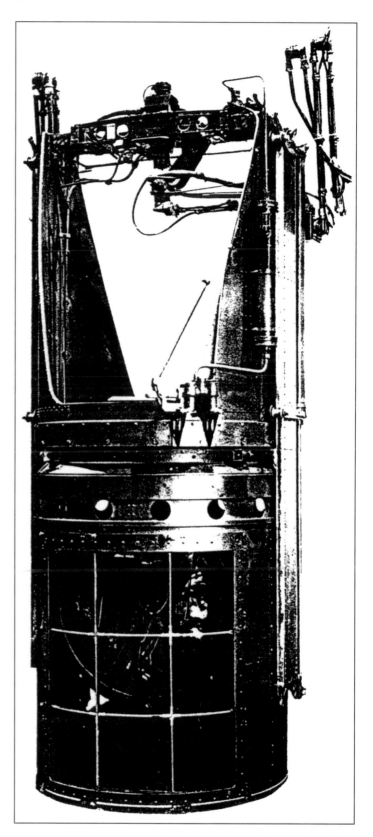

The Leigh Light installation in a turret to be fitted in a DWI (Directional Wireless Installation) Wellington, photographed on 26 January 1941 by Parnell Aircraft Ltd of Tolworth in Surrey. The DWI Wellington was one of those machines fitted with a huge hoop containing a magnetic coil used for exploding magnetic mines; it was made available for the Leigh Light experiment after the coil had been removed.

Author's collection

matters all their own way, for one of these machines was shot down by a Wellington of No. 15 Operational Training Unit five days later. From this time the tempo of the air war over the Bay of Biscay increased dramatically.

In the mid-Atlantic the war continued with increased ferocity, both sides having gained strength. Many of the attacks took place in the so-called 'Atlantic Gap', where the convoys could expect only limited protection from Coastal Command's handful of Liberators. Nevertheless, the U-boats found pickings far less easy than previously. The number of escorts had increased, with usually six warships to a convoy, although this was still fewer than the desired number. More of these vessels were equipped with HF/DF, and many were fitted with new Types 271–273 radar which enabled them to pick up a surfaced U-boat from about 3 miles, even in fog or at night. Information gathered enabled controllers of the Submarine Tracking Room to route some convoys around known wolf-packs.

Depth-charges had become more deadly, filled with the more powerful 'Torpex' and capable of being set to explode at depths of as much as 500ft. A system of refuelling vessels at sea from tankers had been introduced, enabling the escorts to cover the whole journey instead of having to turn back while en route. Rescue ships sailed with the convoys, with the duty of picking up survivors from sunken ships, thus relieving the escorts of this task. Synthetic trainers in Britain had enabled commanders to understand the best methods of combating the U-boats.

By this time the burden of escorting convoys in this critical area was shared roughly equally between the Royal Navy and the Royal Canadian Navy, almost all the American warships having been withdrawn to protect their own convoys. The battles between the naval and air escorts and their attackers resulted in the sinking during July of 98 merchant ships totalling about 487,000 tons, plus 3 totalling 24,000 tons in the South Atlantic, for the loss of 11 U-boats and an Italian submarine.

These events were not without the occasional tragic accident. For instance, the author was an RAF troop deck officer on the liner SS *Rangitiki*, outward bound with convoy WS21 from Liverpool to Durban, when on 31 July 1942 'friendly fire' shot down Sunderland III serial W4025 of 201 Squadron sent from Castle Archdale in Northern Ireland to provide air protection. In the misty early morning the RAF flying boat was mistaken by the gunners for a Focke-Wulf Condor. Eleven of the crew members were killed, with only the rear gunner being picked up by one of the naval escorts.

The pace of mid-Atlantic warfare continued unabated into August, when 96 merchant ships totalling over 508,000 tons were sunk in the North Atlantic and 10 more totalling about 34,000 tons in the South Atlantic, for the loss of 10 U-boats. These figures disguise the fact that many convoys slipped through the danger areas unmolested, and only a few suffered severely. For example, in early August the homeward-bound convoy SC94 was beset by a wolf-pack and lost 11 of its 36 merchant ships, although the escorts succeeded in sinking 2 U-boats. There were still too few escorts to provide the full protection required by the convoys, in spite of the unremitting efforts made by these dedicated seamen.

September provided a similar story, with 95 merchant ships totalling over 473,000 tons sunk in the North Atlantic and 7 more totalling almost 58,000 tons in the South Atlantic, in return for 10 U-boats. The worst loss was the liner *Laconia* of 19,559 tons, torpedoed on 12 September when a little south of the Equator by the Type IXC *U-156* commanded by Korvettenkapitän Werner

A tanker sinking after being torpedoed in the North Atlantic.

Hartenstein. She was carrying about 1,800 Italian prisoners, 160 Polish ex-prisoners and 268 British personnel to Britain, in addition to her crew of 436. Hearing cries in Italian from the water, Hartenstein began rescuing survivors, while displaying a Red Cross flag. He notified Dönitz and then broadcast a message in English appealing for help. Dönitz sent two other U-boats and an Italian submarine to his assistance and the rescue work went on for three days. French warships set out for the scene from Dakar in the Vichy colony of Senegal.

However, on 16 September a B-24D Liberator of the 343rd Bombardment Group arrived from Wideawake airfield, which had been secretly built by the Americans on the British island of Ascension in the South Atlantic. This dropped depth-bombs on an upturned lifeboat, apparently under the impression that it was a U-boat, and also destroyed another lifeboat containing Italian prisoners. Eventually the French warships rescued over a thousand survivors, as a result of Hartenstein's humane action. But the bombing by the US Liberator infuriated Dönitz, who issued orders forbidding any further attempts to rescue survivors of torpedoed ships.

In the month of September the Germans began to take countermeasures against the ASV Mark II radar fitted to RAF anti-submarine aircraft. They had known of its existence for a long time and indeed had fitted a captured set to a Focke-Wulf Condor during the previous year. With the intensification of the war over the Bay of Biscay, something more positive needed to be done to provide a radar device for U-boats, but the German radio industry was too heavily involved in supplying instruments for the Luftwaffe. Accordingly, two French companies in Paris, Metox and Grandin, were ordered to produce a receiver known as the

In the afternoon of 3 September 1942 Whitley V serial Z6978 of 77 Squadron, Bomber Command (on loan to Coastal Command), was on patrol from Chivenor in North Devon when the crew spotted a U-boat on the surface about 180 miles south-west of Land's End. This was the Type VIIC *U-705* from Kiel, under the command of Kapitänleutnant Karl-Horst Horn on its first war cruise. It had already sunk one merchant vessel, the American *Balladier* of 3,279 tons, on 15 August. The Whitley was flown by Flight Sergeant A.A. MacInnes, who dived to 50ft and released depth-charges. Both front and rear gunners opened fire at the men on the conning tower. The U-boat sank with the loss of all 45 hands.

Wing Commander John C. Graham DFC*

R600A in large quantities and at speed. This was able to pick up transmissions on frequencies between 115 and 500 megacycles, in the knowledge that the ASV Mark II transmitted on 176 and 220 megacycles.

This device was known officially as the 'Metox', or more generally as the 'Biscaykreux' (Biscay Cross) after the shape of its aerial, and was immediately successful. The U-boat crews could pick up an approaching aircraft from a distance of over 30 miles – greater than the normal effectiveness of the airborne instrument – and dive before it neared them. Only two sightings were made at night by Leigh Light aircraft over the Bay during September, and the U-boats were able to travel on the surface once more – at least for the time being.

Sinkings continued at a high level in October 1942, with 62 merchant ships totalling almost 400,000 tons lost in the North Atlantic. Another 20 totalling over 148,000 tons were sunk in the South Atlantic, for Dönitz had moved more of his U-boats to the rich pickings off the African coasts. But the number of U-boats sunk rose to 16, 10 of which were the result of the increasingly effective air operations.

On 30 October there was a splendid bonus for British Intelligence when vital material was captured from the Type VIIC *U-559*, commanded by Kapitän-leutnant Hans Heidtmann on its tenth war cruise. This incident did not take place in the North Atlantic but in the Mediterranean, about 60 miles north-east of Port Said. The U-boat was first picked up in the early morning by the radar of a patrolling Sunderland but it crash-dived before the aircraft reached its position.

The destroyer HMS *Hero* soon reached the scene, followed by four more destroyers, HMS *Petard*, HMS *Pakenham*, HMS *Dulverton* and HMS *Hurworth*. These were supported by a Vickers Wellesley of 47 Squadron from Shallufa in Egypt. The first to locate the submerged U-boat with Asdic was HMS *Pakenham*. Attacks with depth-charges began and continued for many hours. These did not seriously damage *U-559* at first but in the late evening the continual blasts coupled with foulness of air and exhaustion of batteries forced the U-boat to the surface.

The sea vents were opened and the men clambered out to surrender, under gunfire and the glare of searchlights. Seven men were lost, and the U-boat did not sink immediately. One officer and four seamen from HMS *Petard* managed to clamber inside, where they recovered a four-rotor Enigma machine and its code books. These were handed to other men in a whaler, while they went back to search for more equipment, but the U-boat suddenly sank, taking two of the men with it. Their sacrifice enabled Bletchley Park to break into the 'Triton' code and decrypt the messages sent by U-boats in the Atlantic.

Another player entered the scene in this month. This was the US Eighth Air Force, which had begun minor operations from England in early August 1942 and was steadily building up its strength and experience. On 21 October 1942 it dispatched 66 B-17 Fortresses and 24 B-24 Liberators in daylight to bomb the U-boat pens in Lorient. Low cloud prevented any worthwhile results on this occasion, but it was the forerunner of the increasingly massive raids which the Eighth Air Force would make against the U-boat ports in western France.

The Anglo-American landings in north-west Africa which started on 8 November caught Dönitz and the other Axis leaders completely by surprise. Over 100 ships transported American troops direct from their home country to land in the Casablanca area of Morocco, entirely without loss. At the same time, an armada of over 250 ships landed British and American troops near Oran in Algeria, having sailed from Britain without loss. Attacks on these convoys were made by U-boats but there were no wolf-packs and such was the strength of the escorts that not a single ship was sunk.

In response, Dönitz diverted some of his boats to the Straits of Gibraltar, the Moroccan coast and the western Mediterranean, but they achieved little for the loss of 7 of their number. Another 6 U-boats were sunk in the North Atlantic during the month, but 83 ships totalling about 508,000 tons were lost, and 10 more totalling almost 59,000 tons were sunk in the South Atlantic. The U-boats were still numerous enough to continue winning the war of attrition by sinking ships at a greater rate than they could be replaced.

November was also the month when Admiral Sir Percy Noble ended his appointment as Commander-in-Chief of Western Approaches and was succeeded by Admiral Sir Max Horton, who was able to build on the achievements of his predecessor. From this time Horton was the person with the task of outwitting Britain's main opponent in the Battle of the Atlantic, Admiral Karl Dönitz. Stormy weather in the North Atlantic in December restricted U-boat operations, but 56 ships totalling 262,000 tons were sunk, with 8 more totalling over 43,000 tons in the South Atlantic. The number of U-boats sunk dropped to 5.

Dönitz began 1943 with a greatly increased strength of 212 operational U-boats, plus another 164 under trials or employed on training. In many ways this was the peak of his U-boat successes. Ominous dark clouds were gathering on the horizon which would affect the course of his campaign. The Third Reich was beginning to experience major reversals under Hitler's conduct of the war. The

Sixth Army was besieged in Stalingrad and would shortly be wiped out by the Russians, with the loss of 278,000 men and their equipment. The British had driven the Panzerarmee out of the Western Desert. Morocco and Algeria were in the hands of the Anglo-Americans, although a great struggle lay ahead in Tunisia. Bomber Command was hammering German cities almost nightly, causing great devastation with its new four-engined bombers carrying increased loads.

In this changed atmosphere the American and British leaders decided to meet at Casablanca in Morocco, in order to decide on a common strategic policy for the remainder of the war. Stalin announced that he would not be present, on the grounds that he was too busy directing his armies in the defeat of the Wehrmacht, but Generalissimo Chiang Kai-shek was in attendance. The discussions took place for ten days from 13 January 1943, and some of the major decisions affected the Battle of the Atlantic. One of the most important outcomes was to accord top priority to the defeat of the U-boats.

This decision did not result in a sudden flow of new aircraft and equipment to Coastal Command, although much was in the pipeline already. However, on 14 January 1943 the Air Officer Commanding Bomber Command, Air Chief Marshal Sir Arthur Harris, received a new directive from the War Cabinet. He was to institute immediately a maximum effort against the French towns which harboured U-boats. In order of priority these were Lorient, St Nazaire, Brest and La Pallice.

During 1942 about 20 per cent of Bomber Command's effort had been directed towards the war at sea, in operations such as minelaying outside ports and raids on German submarine yards such as those at Lübeck and Rostock in the Baltic. But this new directive implied that the techniques of 'area bombing' were now to be carried out against French towns, without regard to civilian casualties. It illustrated the danger that the U-boats were posing to Britain's lifeline across the North Atlantic, but it was a tragedy for the French people. However, not even the heaviest bombs could penetrate the immensely thick layers of concrete which covered the U-boat pens. Bomber Command had failed to destroy these while they were under construction, but now the other facilities provided by these ports were to be destroyed.

A large ocean-going Type IX U-boat, fitted with a single 37-mm anti-aircraft gun.

U-Boot-Archiv, Cuxhaven-Altenbruch

A 105-mm deck gun, as fitted to the larger and longer-range Type IX U-boats. The smaller Type VII U-boats were equipped with 88-mm guns.

Jak P. Mallmann Showell collection

Some of the crew of a U-boat, huddled together for a meal.

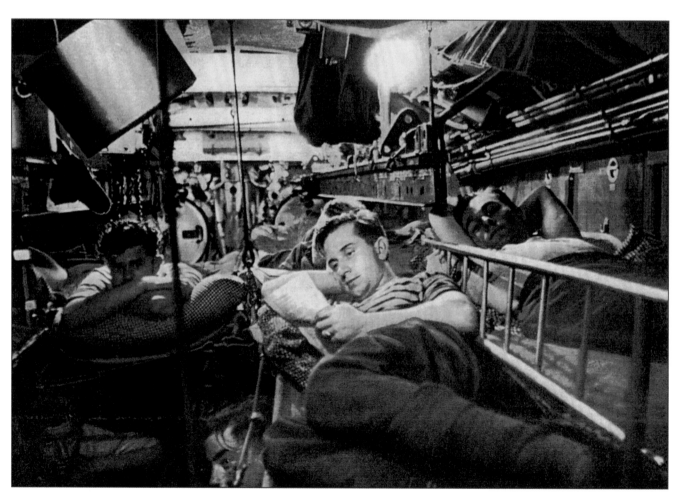

The cramped sleeping quarters in a U-boat.

The central control room in a U-boat, looking forwards. The engine telegraph dials are on the right, with one partially hidden behind the seaman's head. The circular door is in a pressure-resistant bulkhead.

U-Boot-Archiv, Cuxhaven-Altenbruch

The diesel engine room in a U-boat.

U-Boot-Archiv, Cuxhaven-Altenbruch

A torpedoed tanker sinking stern first off the coast of Florida in May 1942. This was the period named 'the second happy time' by U-boat crews.

Author's collection

A merchant ship broken and sinking in the North Atlantic, attended by two tugs from the convoy.

Author's collection

A Consolidated PBY-5 Catalina of the US Navy, photographed on 15 May 1944 by another aircraft fitted with a 'Yagi' aerial for its Air to Surface-Vessel radar. The PBY-5, powered by two Pratt & Whitney R-1830-92 engines of 1,200hp, equipped sixteen squadrons of the US Navy at the time of the attack on Pearl Harbor. It proved outstandingly successful throughout the Second World War.

Bruce Robertson collection

The Martin PBM-1 Mariner was a seven- or eight-seat flying boat, powered by two Wright R-2600-6 Cyclone engines of 1,600hp, which first entered service with the US Navy in April 1941. It could carry 2,000lb of bombs or depth-charges and was armed with eight 0.50-inch machine-guns. Mariners were employed over the Atlantic seaboard on anti-submarine duties. The PBM-3, shown here, was powered by two R-2600-22 Cyclone engines of 1,900hp.

Bruce Robertson collection

The Vought OS2U-1 Kingfisher, powered by a Pratt & Whitney R-985-45 engine of 450hp, was a two-seat floatplane which entered service with the US Navy in August 1940. It was armed with two 0.30-inch machine-guns and could carry two 325lb depth-bombs. Launched from catapults on capital ships and cruisers, it proved successful in the roles of reconnaissance and air–sea rescue. A hundred of these floatplanes were also supplied to the Royal Navy.

Bruce Robertson collection

A crane lifting a gun, possibly of 3-inch or 5-inch calibre, aboard an American merchant vessel as defence against enemy attack in the Atlantic. Machine-guns were also fitted in 'bandstands' on these vessels. The ships' names have been obliterated in this photograph by the censor.

Author's collection

The Consolidated PB2Y-3 Coronado flying boat served in the US Navy as a patrol bomber, powered by four Pratt & Whitney R-1830-88 engines of 2,000hp and armed with eight 0.50-inch machine-guns. Ten were supplied to the RAF in 1943, such as serial JX470 shown here with beaching gear at the Saunders-Roe location at Beaumaris in Anglesey. However, the ten flying boats were rejected by Coastal Command and converted into freight and passenger carriers. They were taken on charge by 231 Squadron and served mainly on the North Atlantic route between Scotland and Newfoundland.

Bruce Robertson collection

A Lake class cutter of the US Coastguard, one of ten taken into service by the Royal Navy in 1941. They were converted and renamed Lulworth class sloops.

Author's collection

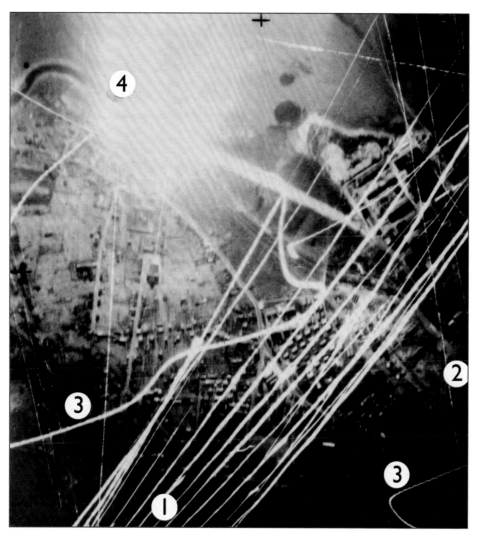

Flak at night over the U-boat base at St Nazaire, photographed during a low-level bombing attack by RAF Coastal Command. (1) Intense light flak. (2) Tracer bullets. (3) Searchlight beams hunting the bombers. (4) Fire in the dock area.

Author's collection

Matilda tanks being loaded aboard merchant vessels at a British port before being taken in convoy to North Russia. These tanks were heavily armoured but slow and lightly armed.

Author's collection

A low-level photograph of the battleship *Tirpitz* in Aasfjord, near Trondheim, taken in February 1942 by a Spitfire of No. 1 Photographic Reconnaissance Unit of Coastal Command. Other vessels around her and camouflage netting draped between her port side and the shore were intended to break up her outline from the air.

Author's collection

The results of the combined operation of
28 March 1942 on St Nazaire when the
destroyer HMS *Campbeltown* (formerly the
USS *Buchanan*) rammed the outer lock gate at
the entrance to the Bassin de Penhouet at (A)
and Commandos stormed the docks. The
concrete dam is at (B) and damage to the
machine house is at (C).

Author's collection

A Tribal class destroyer on the alert for enemy bombers, probably Focke-Wulf Fw200 Condors operating from Norway or south-west France. It is fitted with quadruple 0.5-inch guns in the foreground and quadruple 2-pounders aft of the funnel.

Author's collection

A Royal Navy lieutenant on an Atlantic convoy, wearing protective gear against bomb flashes, giving a running commentary on enemy air attacks to the crew below.

Author's collection

The explosion of bombs dropped by Focke-Wulf Fw200 Condors on an Atlantic convoy, photographed from an escorting cruiser of the Royal Navy.

Author's collection

Patches of oil burning on the surface of the sea, probably after a tanker had been torpedoed and set on fire.

Author's collection

Condor over Norway
by Mark Postlethwaite GAvA
   Focke-Wulf Fw 200C-4 Condor,
F8+FL, of 3./Kampfgeschwader 40
stationed at Trondheim-Vaernes in
Norway, flying over a fjord in March
1942. This long-distance bomber is
equipped with a nose-mounted
FuG 200 Howentwiel radar
antenna, an HDL 151 turret with a
15-mm cannon on top of the
fuselage near the pilot, as well as a
dorsal position further aft for a
gunner with an MG15 machine-gun.

The destroyer HMS *Onslow*, of 1,540 tons displacement, was armed with four 4.7-inch guns and was capable of 37 knots. When photographed here, she was fitted with MF/DF on the bridge front, HF/DF Type S25B on the mainmast, Type 291 radar on the head of the foremast, Type 272 radar on the foremast and Type 285 radar on the director. She was responsible for the depth-charging and sinking of the Type VIIC *U-589* on 14 September 1942. She won fame on 31 December 1942 during the Battle of the Barents Sea when she was one of five destroyers escorting convoy JW51B to North Russia which held off the pocket battleship *Lützow*, the heavy cruiser *Admiral Hipper* and six German destroyers until two light cruisers of the Royal Navy arrived. Her commander, Captain R. St V. Sherbrooke, was wounded in the action and was later awarded the Victoria Cross.

Oscar Parkes Society

An Atlantic convoy steaming in line ahead into the sunset, with a balloon as protection against enemy bombers, viewed from the lookout position on an escorting destroyer.

Author's collection

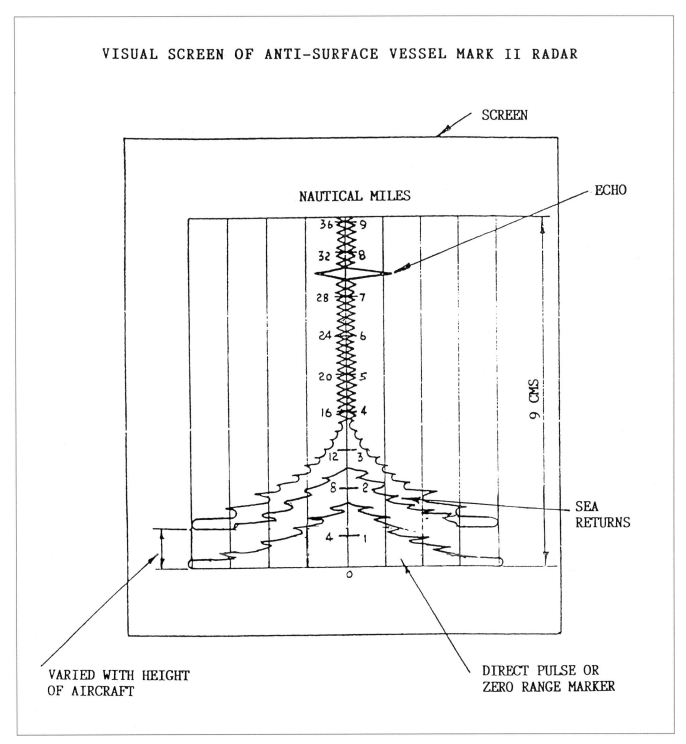

Visual Screen of Air to Surface-Vessel Mark II Radar

This example shows an object ahead, picked up slightly to starboard by the forward aerials. The instrument could be switched to short range (mile intervals), medium range (4 mile intervals), or long range (10 mile intervals), as shown on the vertical scale. Maximum range was about 90 miles.

Boeing B-17C Flying Fortresses were flown to Britain in the spring of 1941 for modification to RAF requirements. The first was serial AN518 shown in this photograph. Fortresses first entered service in May 1941 with 90 Squadron of Bomber Command, based at West Raynham in Norfolk, but were soon considered more suitable for Coastal Command.

Author's collection

Boeing Fortress IIA serial FK186 of 220 Squadron in May 1943, flying near its base on Benbecula in the Outer Hebrides.

Imperial War Museum TR1084

The navigator of a Consolidated Liberator being
ferried across the North Atlantic from North America
to Britain. The crew of this aircraft included RAF and
RCAF personnel as well as American civilians.

Author's collection

A Liberator I of the RAF, with armament, armour plating and self-sealing fuel tanks. No. 120 Squadron at Nutts Corner in Northern Ireland was the first to receive these machines, in June 1941. It was armed with four 0.50-inch machine-guns, operated manually in nose, tail and waist positions, plus four 20-mm cannons in a gun pack below the fuselage. It was also fitted with Air to Surface-Vessel radar, with aerials mounted above the fuselage as well as on the wings and in the nose. It was the forerunner of the land-based aircraft which closed the 'Atlantic Gap' where hitherto U-boats had been able to operate with impunity from air attack.

Author's collection

An RAF Liberator over a tanker in the North Atlantic, part of a convoy bringing supplies to Britain.

Author's collection

Das Verdammte Licht! by Mark Postlethwaite GAvA
  A Type VII U-boat illuminated in mid-1942 at night in
the Bay of Biscay by a Vickers Wellington VIII of
172 Squadron operating from Chivenor in North
Devon. The aircraft was armed with depth-charges and
fitted with Mark III Air to Surface-Vessel radar
together with a Leigh Light which could be lowered in
a 'dustbin' turret below the fuselage. These new
devices made U-boats vulnerable to attack from the
air at night and severely hindered their method of
recharging batteries by sailing on the surface to and
from the mid-Atlantic. The U-boat men hated this
British invention and referred to it as 'that damned
light!'

Squadron Leader Humphrey de Verde 'Sammy' Leigh, the inventor of the airborne searchlight
that bore his name, photographed in 1942.

Author's collection

Wellington Mark XIV, serial HF167, with a chin radome for Air to Surface-Vessel radar under
the nose and a retractable Leigh Light in the lowered position.

Author's collection

A stick of depth-charges exploding across the Italian submarine *Luigi Torelli* soon after 07.12 hours on 7 June 1942, north of Santander in Spain. They were dropped by Sunderland II serial W3994 of 10 (RAAF) Squadron, flown from Mount Batten in Devon under the captaincy of Pilot Officer Thomas A. Egerton.

Author's collection

The *Luigi Torelli*, beached near Santander in Spain after suffering extensive damage caused by depth-charges dropped by a Leigh Light Wellington of 172 Squadron and two Sunderlands of 10 (RAAF) Squadron. The photograph was taken at 18.50 hours on 8 June 1942 by a Hudson of 53 Squadron flown from St Eval in Cornwall by the commanding officer, Wing Commander James A. Leggate.

Author's collection

Seamen from a warship of the Royal Navy rescuing the only remaining survivor on a life-raft from a vessel torpedoed by a U-boat. Two officers on the raft were found to be dead.

Author's collection

A solitary survivor on an upturned lifeboat, waving thankfully to his rescuers.

Author's collection

A lifeboat and life-raft, after survivors had been rescued.

Author's collection

THESE MEN WENT THROUGH **HELL** *for* **YOU**

FOR 13 DAYS THESE MEN WERE ADRIFT IN AN OPEN BOAT. THEIR SHIP HAD BEEN SUNK BY A GERMAN RAIDER IN THE ATLANTIC . . . THERE WERE 82 MEN CROWDED INTO A BOAT BUILT TO HOLD 50 . . . ONE OF THE BOATS FINALLY REACHED SÃO LUIZ, BRAZIL, WHERE THE MEN FELL EXHAUSTED ON THE BEACH . . . .

GIVE US THE SHIPS WE'LL DELIVER THE GOODS!

BUILDING SHIPS LIKE THIS WILL MAKE YOU AND THE NAVY AN UNBEATABLE TEAM

The men of the Royal Navy and Merchant Navy ask you to give every ounce of effort to speed up production. Give them the weapons to fight back at the Germans and protect the women and children of Britain from what has happened in the countries now occupied by the enemy.

From America and our Dominions we are obtaining planes, war materials and vital foods. The Merchant Navy, convoyed by the Royal Navy, are maintaining our life line and with your help they will continue to keep this country supplied with the necessities of life and the weapons to beat Hitler and his gang. Every worker engaged on producing even the smallest nut or bolt needed to complete a ship is doing his bit to win this war.

The Navy is depending on you to replace the ships which are being lost. Production must be increased. There is no time to be lost. Every hour wasted is an hour gained by the Germans in their attempt to sweep us off the high seas and thus pave the way for an invasion of this island.

Warwork News No. 8 1941

ISSUED BY THE ADMIRALTY

PRINTED FOR H.M. STATIONERY OFFICE BY FOSH & CROSS LTD., LONDON. 51-8990.

Public Record Office: INF 13/213/50

In the mid-morning of 23 June 1942 the Type VIIC *U-753*, commanded by Korvettenkapitän Alfred Manhardt von Mannstein, was attacked about 350 miles west of the Gironde Estuary by Whitley VII serial Z9135 of 58 Squadron, flown from St Eval by Flight Sergeant W. Jones. Six depth-charges were dropped, four of which were seen to straddle the diving U-boat. It reappeared after about five minutes and an exchange of gunfire took place, in which the Whitley was hit in the bomb bay but the German gunners were seen to collapse. The U-boat then submerged once more. It managed to reach La Pallice and underwent extensive repairs, but was sunk in the North Atlantic on 15 May 1943 from an uncertain cause. There were no survivors.

Author's collection

Officer prisoners from German U-boats and Italian submarines arriving at an English port, blindfolded for security reasons.

Author's collection

Admiral Sir Max Horton, Commander-in-Chief of Western Approaches, in his underground office at Derby House in Liverpool. He was appointed in November 1942 after specialising in submarine warfare, and then became the main adversary to Grand Admiral Karl Dönitz in the Battle of the Atlantic.

Author's collection

The quick-firing 88-mm gun, with a watertight tampion on its muzzle, on the deck of either the Type VIIC *U-71* or *U-72*. Both periscopes are raised and there is a loudspeaker on the top of the conning tower in front of the flagpole.

U-Boot-Archiv, Cuxhaven-Altenbruch

The interior of Bunker Keroman II at Lorient, Germany's largest U-boat base on the Biscay coast, with a Type IX U-boat in dry dock.

U-Boot-Archiv, Cuxhaven-Altenbruch

This Whitley V serial Z6795 of No. 10 Operational Training Unit was fished from the sea by the Germans after ditching on the coast near Brest on 21 September 1942. The unit was based at Abingdon in Berkshire but a detachment had been sent to St Eval in Cornwall to gain operational experience and help in the war against the U-boats. It was on a 12-hour patrol in the Bay of Biscay, under the captaincy of a New Zealander, Pilot Officer Neyeille J. Mundell, but weather conditions proved extremely adverse and the machine probably ran out of fuel. All six men in the crew were taken prisoner, although Mundell was reported as wounded, possibly in the ditching.

A. Richard Chapman collection

A westbound convoy in the North Atlantic, photographed from a Boeing Flying Fortress of Coastal Command in October 1942.

Author's collection

The Three Power Conference at Casablanca in January 1943, during which the relative proportion of military effort against Germany and Japan was settled. One of the main priorities was the destruction of the German U-boat arm. Bottom row, left to right: Generalissimo Chiang Kai-shek; President Roosevelt; Winston Churchill; Madame Chiang Kai-shek. Top row: General Chang Chen; Lieutenant-General Ling Wei; Lieutenant-General B.B. Somervell; Lieutenant-General J.W. Stilwell; General H.A.P. Arnold; Field Marshal Sir John Dill; Admiral Lord Louis Mountbatten; Major-General Carton de Wiart.

Author's collection

CHAPTER FIVE

UNHAPPY TIMES FOR U-BOATS

Sinkings of merchant ships in Atlantic waters diminished in January 1943, with the onset of winter storms. In all, only 27 vessels were lost in the North Atlantic, totalling about 172,500 tons, while 3 totalling about 16,000 tons were sunk in the South Atlantic. U-boat losses were also low, with only 5 sunk in these waters. Much of the month was spent battling against Atlantic storms instead of the enemy.

However, there was a notable change in the German high command. On 30 January 1943 Karl Dönitz was accorded the rank of Grossadmiral and placed in charge of the entire Kriegsmarine, thus succeeding Grossadmiral Eric Raedar, who resigned after a disagreement with Hitler. In spite of the increased weight of his duties, Dönitz retained command of the U-boat arm, a position in which he was without doubt the foremost expert of his country. There was also a change in the RAF's Coastal Command when, on 5 February 1943, Air Marshal Sir John Slessor was moved from No. 5 Group of Bomber Command to take over from Air Chief Marshal Sir Philip Joubert de la Ferté. He assumed command in far more favourable circumstances than his predecessor had endured for much of his 19 months in office. There were 54 squadrons and 4 flights in Coastal Command, comprising 858 aircraft. Not all of these were dedicated to anti-submarine warfare, such as the coastal strike squadrons, the photo-reconnaissance squadrons and the air–sea rescue squadrons. However, 3 of the others were equipped with Catalinas, 4 with Liberators, 9 with Sunderlands, 3 with Fortresses, 2 with Halifaxes, 5 with Wellingtons, 3 with Hudsons and 2 with Whitleys. These squadrons were to play a crucial part in the Battle of the Atlantic during the next few months.

Air Chief Marshal Sir Arthur Harris of Bomber Command carried out immediately the instructions passed to him on 14 January 1943 from the Casablanca Conference. A heavy raid against Lorient took place on the same night. It was repeated on the following night and raids continued at intervals until by the end of February almost all the buildings in the port had been destroyed. The bombers then turned their attention to St Nazaire. Most of the

French residents in these ports had fled their homes, so that civilian casualties were fairly light.

The US Eighth Air Force also took part in this campaign, with daylight attacks on Lorient, Brest and St Nazaire. However, it became recognised that all these Allied bombardments were having little effect on the immensely thick roofs of the U-boat pens and that it would be more profitable to divert much of the effort against U-boat construction yards in German ports. Bomber Command switched its night attacks to these targets, although the US Eighth Air Force continued to carry out some daylight raids against the French ports.

The U-boats sank 42 ships totalling 289,000 tons in the North Atlantic during February 1943, plus 4 totalling 22,000 tons in the South Atlantic. They were still finding their easiest targets in the 'Atlantic Gap', out of reach of air escorts. Early in the month the eastbound convoy SC118 was beset by 20 U-boats, which sank 13 vessels out of 63 for the loss of 3 of their number. Later in the same month, the westbound convoy ON166 lost 14 ships while only a single U-boat was sunk. But the total number of U-boats destroyed in the Atlantic during February rose sharply to 19, including 10 from the air.

A higher proportion of merchant ships went to the bottom in March, with 82 totalling over 476,000 tons in the North Atlantic and 8 totalling over 61,000 tons in the South Atlantic. Two eastbound convoys were mauled, both in the 'Atlantic Gap'. Convoy SC121 lost 13 ships when set upon by 38 U-boats, while none of the attackers was sunk. Convoy HX228 from Halifax fared better, although 8 merchant vessels were sunk in return for 2 U-boats. Encounters between convoys and U-boats lessened in the last eleven days of the month, since both sides were affected by fierce storms which raged in the Atlantic. Merchant

An 88-mm gun fitted to the Type VIIC *U-960* in February 1943, labelled 'Heini' on its starboard side. At this stage the boat was also armed with twin 20-mm cannon. The 88-mm gun was removed in July 1943 and replaced with another set of twin 20-mm cannon. The four cannon were removed in February 1944 and replaced with a single 37-mm gun.

Fregattenkapitän a.D. Günther Heinrich

The highly successful escort carrier USS *Bogue*, which carried a composite squadron of Grumman TBF Avengers and Grumman F4F Wildcats. From May 1943 these aircraft were responsible for sinking eight U-boats in the North Atlantic. They also sank the Japanese submarine *I-52* on 24 June 1944, west of the Cape Verde Islands, when this was acting as a blockade runner to Lorient.

Author's collection

vessels laden with trucks and other war material were forced to heave-to in gales that reached almost hurricane force. Some became scattered from the convoys and a few capsized and sank from the force of the elements. These conditions also affected the U-boats, which could not operate on the surface to reach their targets. Nevertheless, a total of 13 U-boats were sunk in the Atlantic during the month, 8 of which were from the air.

There were several reasons for this increase in U-boat sinkings, and indeed they constituted harbingers of things to come. One was the adoption of a recommendation by Professor Patrick Blackett, who had moved from working with the RAF's Coastal Command to the Admiralty in January 1942. This involved increasing the number of ships in a convoy from an average of 32 to 54, with a commensurate increase in the number of naval escorts from 6 to 9. Air cover was easier to arrange with fewer convoys, and the U-boats found such defences far more difficult and dangerous to penetrate.

Another improvement in the Atlantic convoys was the welcome addition in March 1943 of the escort carrier USS *Bogue*. This carried a composite squadron of Avengers and Wildcats which normally operated in pairs, the former to drop depth-charges or a homing torpedo (known for security reasons as a Mark 24 mine) while the latter suppressed any flak from the U-boat with its six 0.50-inch machine-guns. Several of these American-built carriers had been operating with the Royal Navy and its Fleet Air Arm for some months, although they had been busy with the landings in North Africa and the convoys to North Russia. In April 1943 these carriers would be able to combine with destroyers to form Support Groups; sailing with the Atlantic convoys, they helped to transform the situation in mid-Atlantic.

Another advantage was gained by the introduction of a new weapon on some of the naval escorts. Known as a 'Hedgehog', it consisted of a multi-barrelled

The Grumman TBF Avenger was a carrier-borne torpedo-bomber with a crew of three. The TBF-3, such as the example fitted with rocket rails in this photograph, was powered by a Wright Cyclone R-2600-20 engine of 1,750hp and was armed with two forward-firing 0.50-inch machine-guns and two more in dorsal and ventral positions. It could carry an ordnance of up to 2,000lb – a torpedo, bombs or rockets. The Royal Navy received about 400 Avengers, mostly under Lease-Lend arrangements.

Bruce Robertson collection

An American Mark 19 homing torpedo and two depth-bombs carried in a Grumman TBF Avenger of the US Navy.

US National Archives 80-G-373115 via Roger Hayward

mortar, mounted on the bow of a ship, which fired a pattern of 24 small bombs about 200 yards *ahead* of the ship at a diving U-boat. Each bomb weighed 65lb and was filled with Torpex high explosive. It was armed with a contact fuse and thus only exploded if it hit the U-boat, causing almost certain destruction. The device did not work well in heavy seas and had suffered from some teething problems in late 1942, but from the following March it began to account for several U-boats.

Some of the air escorts had been fitted with a new radar. This was the new Air to Surface-Vessel Mark III (ASV Mark III), a centimetric device which displayed echoes by means of a revolving trace on the screen of a cathode ray tube. It was first supplied to the Leigh Light Wellingtons of 172 Squadron in March 1943, and other squadrons soon followed. Of course, it was a considerable advance on the ASV Mark II and moreover used frequencies outside the coverage of the Metox search receiver carried by U-boats.

German Intelligence (B-Dienst) was already aware of this invention. ASV Mark III was a maritime version of the H2S device which had been supplied to some squadrons of Bomber Command early in the year. On 2 February 1943 a Stirling bomber fitted with an H2S had been shot down over Rotterdam. This was examined with great interest and considerable surprise by German electronics experts, who quickly realised that a similar radar set could be employed against U-boats. This seemed to be confirmed on 3 March 1943 when Wellington serial MP505 of 172 Squadron was shot down over the Bay of Biscay by the Type VIIC *U-333*, after illumination at night with a Leigh Light. The commander of the U-boat, Oberleutnant Werner Schaff, reported that his attacker must have been fitted with a new radar instrument, since its approach had not been picked up by the Metox receiver. The German experts began to develop a countermeasure, which they codenamed 'Naxos', but their Telefunken Company had difficulty producing the crystal detectors required for this instrument. For the time being, no Naxos receivers were available for U-boats.

The operational headquarters of the U-boat arm for the west were in a requisitioned house in the Avenue Maréchal Maumoury in Paris. Dönitz's head of operations, Konteradmiral Eberhard Godt, was in charge of day-to-day business and also commanded the U-boat arm when his superior officer was engaged in other matters. These two high-ranking naval officers were backed by a small team of experienced U-boat officers, each responsible for different areas of operation. There were also a number of specialised intelligence officers who had had some success in breaking the British codes used for convoy instructions in the early months of the war, and occasionally enjoyed success on later occasions.

When this team understood that an Allied convoy was en route, they directed a wolf-pack of U-boats to form a line at right angles to its track. The U-boat commanders maintained strict radio silence at this time, but as soon as a convoy was sighted they notified the Paris headquarters of its position, with numbers of vessels, course and speed. The headquarters staff then sprang into action, sending signals to other U-boats in the patrol line and directing them to the target area. When three U-boats were in position, the attack could begin.

It is perhaps surprising that the officers in the U-boat headquarters did not detect the ease with which they were able to make interceptions of convoys in the months after the four-wheel rotor was introduced in the Enigma machines in February 1942, by comparison with the difficulty they had experienced from the end of October 1941. This would have led them to the suspicion that the British had been able to decrypt the signals sent by the three-rotor Enigma. Unknown to them, the

Mine Layers   Sir Muirhead Bone

War Pictures
BY BRITISH ARTISTS

NATIONAL GALLERY
Trafalgar Square

WEEKDAYS: 10 A.M. TO 6 P.M. OR DUSK. SUNDAYS: 2 P.M. TO 6 P.M. OR DUSK

ADMISSION FREE

Government Code and Cipher School had been decrypting their earlier messages, and was able to do so again from October 1942. Streams of dispatch riders on motor bicycles arrived at Bletchley Park every day, bearing sealed packages containing German messages intercepted by the ten 'Y' Service stations in Britain, mostly in the east of the country. These were passed to the hundreds of young ladies in the Women's Naval Air Service (Wrens) who were sworn to absolute secrecy and worked on the electro-magnetic 'bombes' at Bletchley Park and nearby units, which decrypted these messages. Their hours of work were long, monotonous and gruelling, but even though they could not have fully understood its purpose, they were buoyed by the knowledge that it was of supreme national importance. Not a single secret was divulged by the thousands who worked on this task throughout the war.

The decrypted messages were translated into English and copies of those which related to the U-boat war were passed to the Submarine Tracking Room at the Admiralty. Together with the information forthcoming from the naval escorts equipped with HF/DF, these 'Ultra secret' messages (now released by the Public Record Office at Kew) enabled the Tracking Room to plot the positions of U-boats with more accuracy than German U-boat headquarters in Paris could. This was indeed the 'goose that laid the golden eggs without cackling', as secretly described by Winston Churchill, which did so much to shorten the war and achieve victory for the Allies.

The storms which had affected both convoys and U-boats during the latter part of March 1943 continued into the first few days of April. There was also a short remission for the convoys since many U-boats had returned to French ports for service and rearming. Only one wolf-pack remained in the North Atlantic at the beginning of the month and this intercepted the eastbound convoy HX231 from Halifax. Three merchant ships were sunk, but the encounter was not favourable for the attackers, for one was sunk by a Liberator of 120 Squadron on 5 April and on the following day another was sunk by a Liberator of 86 Squadron. But three other ships which straggled from the convoy were also sunk.

At about the time of this incident, a fresh stream of U-boats began to enter the North Atlantic from French and German ports. In all, 98 sailed during April 1943. Two of them were sunk in the Bay of Biscay by patrolling aircraft. Another was depth-charged by the coastguard cutter USS *Spencer* when attempting to attack Convoy HX233 and was destroyed by gunfire when it came to the surface. Other U-boats which attempted to attack the outward-bound Convoy ONS4 were thwarted when they found that it was supported by an American-built escort carrier. This was HMS *Biter*, the first of those to operate with the Royal Navy in the North Atlantic. She carried Swordfish armed with up to 1,500lb of depth-charges which were quite capable of putting paid to a U-boat if dropped correctly. Other Swordfish were fitted with a strengthened lower wing carrying eight rockets armed with 25-lb armour-piercing warheads capable of blasting lethal holes in an unfortunate U-boat.

Sinkings in the North Atlantic during April dropped dramatically to 39 merchant ships totalling about 235,000 tons, while only one, a vessel of 7,000 tons, was lost in the South Atlantic. In return, 13 U-boats were sunk, 8 from the air, 4 from depth-charges and the other from a mine. In addition, an Italian submarine was sunk in the South Atlantic by an American aircraft. It was not a happy result for Dönitz, who began to realise that the scales of the Battle of the Atlantic were weighted against him.

The month of May 1943 brought the campaign to a climax. This was the time when all the Allied endeavours came together in sufficient force to defeat the U-

In the morning of 19 April 1943 Sunderland III serial JM676 of 461 (RAAF) Squadron was on patrol in the Bay of Biscay, flown by Flying Officer R. de V. Gipps on his first operational sortie as captain. After a radar contact, a conning tower and part of the deck of a U-boat were sighted at 10.35 hours, before disappearing. Gipps dropped markers and resumed the patrol. Another radar contact was made at 11.24 hours and Gipps attacked with six depth-charges. The U-boat sank horizontally but then the stern rose before disappearing vertically. The crew reported seeing a sailor in the water. This U-boat was the Type XB *U-119*, a large minelayer, but it was not seriously damaged. It was sunk on 24 June 1943 north-west of Cape Finisterre by the sloop HMS *Starling*.

Author's collection

boats in the Battle of the Atlantic – the intelligence from the Submarine Tracking Room, the larger convoys with increased numbers of escorts, the Support Groups with their escort carriers and destroyers, the other naval escorts with HF/DF, new radar and new weaponry, the long-range aircraft in larger numbers and the shorter-range aircraft with Leigh Lights, some equipped with the new ASV Mark III. The 'Atlantic Gap' had been closed and nowhere was safe for U-boats in the Atlantic.

At the beginning of May 130 U-boats were at sea and 101 of these were on the North Atlantic routes. This was the highest number achieved in the entire war. One wolf-pack was in position south-west of Iceland, another north-east of Newfoundland, a third to the south of this position, while a fourth was athwart the route to Gibraltar. The three northern packs were seeking the three eastbound convoys of which German Intelligence was aware, HX235, SC127 and SC128. But Bletchley Park knew of their intentions and the three convoys were routed around the menace of U-boats ahead.

One U-boat in the most northerly wolf-pack had already found the outward-bound Convoy ONS5 on 28 April, but the U-boats which closed in for the kill achieved no sinkings against strong protection, while two of their number were damaged. However, the convoy became scattered in a full gale, with low visibility and the presence of drifting icebergs. Two U-boats collided on 3 May and were sunk. The two northerly wolf-packs then formed into a single group and the merchant ships in Convoy ONS5 with their escorts sailed into this on 4 May. Six ships were sunk during the following night, but a U-boat was destroyed by a Canso (Catalina) of 5 (RCAF) Squadron from Newfoundland. Five more merchant ships were sunk during the following day but the attackers paid a heavy price. HF/DF and radar played an important part in their destruction while a fog concealed much of the convoy. Three U-boats were sunk by depth-charges from the naval escorts, plus one by a Hedgehog and one by ramming.

This was a notable victory for the naval escorts, which had reached a pitch of efficiency with their tactics. It was a defeat for Dönitz, who broke off the unprofitable action with Convoy ONS5 and withdrew the remaining U-boats on 6 May. But far worse was to follow. Two more U-boats were picked off by aircraft on 7 May in the Bay of Biscay. Another was sunk on 11 May by a combined air–sea operation near Convoy OS47. The Swordfish from HMS *Biter* attacked another on the following day while escorting Convoy HX237, and this was finished off by depth-charges from a destroyer. Another U-boat was lost on this day, probably after having been damaged by a Canso of a Canadian Squadron four days earlier while attacking Convoy SC128. A Liberator damaged another with a homing torpedo on the next day while it was attempting to attack Convoy HX237; the U-boat was attacked again by a Sunderland before being depth-charged and finished off by a destroyer. Another U-boat which approached this convoy was sunk on 13 May in a combined operation by a Sunderland and two frigates. A Catalina of a US squadron sank yet another U-boat on this day, by means of a homing torpedo, when it was trying to attack Convoy ONS7. Convoy SC129 came under attack by U-boats on 15 May but one U-boat was destroyed by a Halifax. Another was sunk with all hands off Florida by a Cuban sub-chaser on the same day, after being spotted by an aircraft of the US Navy.

The month of misery for U-boats continued. A Halifax sank one in the Bay of Biscay on 16 May, while an Italian submarine was also lost in the same area for uncertain reasons. A US destroyer accounted for another U-boat north-west of Madeira on the same day. Yet another was sunk by the frigate HMS *Swale* on the

The Type IXB *U-109*, commanded by Oberleutnant zur See Joachim Schramm, left Lorient on 28 April 1943 on its ninth war cruise. It was attacked east of the Azores on 4 May by Liberator V serial FL955 of 86 Squadron, flown from Aldergrove in Northern Ireland by Pilot Officer J.C. Green. Four depth-charges straddled the U-boat, resulting in wreckage and a large patch of oil rising to the surface. There were no survivors.

Author's collection

night of 16/17 May while it was attempting to attack Convoy ONS7 off
Newfoundland. In the morning of 17 May a U-boat was scuttled off the coast of
Brazil after a combined operation by a US aircraft and two US destroyers.
Another was sunk south of Iceland on this day, depth-charged by a Hudson from
Reykjavik.

Convoy SC130 was attacked by U-boats near Newfoundland on the night of
18/19 May, but one was destroyed by bombs from Hedgehogs fitted to two
frigates of the Royal Navy. A Hudson from Iceland accounted for a U-boat near
this convoy in the afternoon of the next day. Yet another was lost on the same
day near the convoy, for reasons which cannot be fully established. A Liberator
from Iceland disposed of another close to this convoy on 20 May. It should be
recorded that Convoy SC130 remained unscathed while all this activity was
going on around it.

The destruction of U-boats continued. The escort carrier USS *Bogue* scored its
first success on 22 May while forming part of a Support Group for Convoy
ON184, by sinking a U-boat about 600 miles south-east of Greenland with a
combination of Avengers and Wildcats. Not to be outdone, on the following day
the American-built escort carrier HMS *Archer*, escorting Convoy SC130, sent
rocket-firing Swordfish together with Martlets to sink another U-boat about 670
miles south-east of Greenland. On the same day an Italian submarine was sunk
north-east of the Azores by Royal Navy destroyers.

The accumulated events of the month were too much for Dönitz. The sinkings
of his U-boats were proving greater than his ability to replace them and their
valuable crews. On 24 May he ordered all U-boats in the North Atlantic to
withdraw 'with all possible caution' to a safer area south-west of the Azores. He
admitted in his diary that Germany had lost the Battle of the Atlantic.

But the miseries of the month were not yet over for the German commander.
On 25 May a US Catalina operating from Iceland sank another U-boat about
110 miles south-east of the island. On the following day a frigate and a corvette
of the Royal Navy, escorting Convoy KX10, sank another U-boat about 300
miles west of Cape Finisterre in Spain. A Liberator from Iceland sank a U-boat
360 miles south-west of Greenland on 28 May, while providing cover for Convoy
HX240. The last day of the month brought two more sinkings, both in the Bay
of Biscay. Dönitz had ordered his U-boats to remain on the surface and fight
back against air attack. One was sunk en route to the Atlantic from Brest by a
Halifax and two Sunderlands, while the other was sunk by a Sunderland when
outward bound from St Nazaire.

This dreadful month had cost Dönitz 38 U-boats and 2 Italian submarines
sunk in the Atlantic, plus 3 more U-boats in the Mediterranean. In addition,
several U-boats limped back to French bases in crippled condition, with the crews
lucky to have survived the terrifying experience of relentless depth-charging.
Sinkings of Allied merchant vessels during the month plummeted to 34 ships
totalling about 164,000 tons in the North Atlantic and 6 totalling about 41,000
tons in the South Atlantic. Dönitz's only consolation was that his relatively small
force might continue to tie up a huge amount of Allied resources until the end of
the war.

Thus 24 May 1943 is the date when the Battle of the Atlantic was won by the
Allies. This date has not entered the public consciousness to the same extent as
the winning of the Battle of Britain on 15 September 1940, but it is of equivalent
importance. As with the Battle of Britain, the conflict did not end on that day
and in fact continued for a long period. But after this date merchant ships and

A Consolidated Liberator fitted with rockets by the Aeroplane & Armament Experimental Establishment at Boscombe Down in Wiltshire for possible service with Coastal Command. Photographed on 16 May 1943, it has a Leigh Light under the starboard wing and is fitted with Air to Surface-Vessel Mark II radar.

Bruce Robertson collection

troopships were able to stream across the Atlantic, not with impunity but with a much higher degree of safety. The date established Britain as the 'unsinkable aircraft carrier' from which the liberation of western Europe would be achieved.

The month of June 1943 marked the point when the shipbuilding programme was able to turn out more vessels than were being sunk. America was, of course, the great industrial powerhouse which achieved this objective. The American Maritime Commission had designated eighteen new yards for the construction of the 'Liberty' ships, each of 7,176 tons gross and with a range of 17,000 miles at a cruising speed of 11 knots. They were built in prefabricated sections and welded together in the yards with extraordinary speed. President Roosevelt, a former navy man, called them 'ships built by the mile and chopped off by the yard'. Although not particularly elegant, they served their purpose superbly. Over 200 of them were turned out in 1943, at an average rate of 42 days per ship. They were not the only ships produced in America but they carried immense quantities of supplies to Britain, North Africa and Russia.

The great liners employed as troopships constituted another success in the North Atlantic. The Cunarders *Queen Elizabeth* of 83,675 tons, the *Queen Mary* of 81,235 tons and the *Aquitania* of 44,776 tons had been pressed into service, as had the French *Ile de France* of 43,450 tons and the Dutch *Nieuw Amsterdam*. These brought hundreds of thousands of American troops across the waters, sailing independently at speeds of about 28 knots. They were packed with troops for their relatively short journeys, the *Queen Elizabeth* alone being capable of carrying about 15,000 men. They were 10 knots faster than the maximum speed of any U-boat and not even the naval escorts could keep up with them. None of them fell victim to any U-boat or enemy aircraft.

With the withdrawal of the U-boats from the North Atlantic, the month of June 1943 was the quietest on record. Only 4 merchant ships were sunk in these waters, totalling about 19,000 tons, while 5 more with a total of about 12,000 tons were sunk in the South Atlantic. But a far heavier toll was taken of the U-boats, which lost 16 of their number plus an Italian submarine. Five of these U-boats were sunk in the Bay of Biscay, where early in the month Dönitz had ordered that they sail on the surface in daylight hours in groups, using their combined flak guns to bring down attacking aircraft. The 88-mm deck gun on each U-boat was removed and the anti-aircraft guns were increased to two quadruple-barrelled 20-mm guns plus a single 37-mm gun. This was a challenge to the RAF's No. 19 Group, which covered the Bay of Biscay. It had a strength of 19 RAF operational squadrons, with 2 American Liberator squadrons also under its control. As many as five U-boats sailed together, but this did not deter the RAF and USAAF crews, who attacked in the face of intense fire, resulting in fierce battles.

A 0.50-inch machine-gun fitted as armament on a passenger liner converted for carrying American troops and supplies to Britain or North-West Africa.

Author's collection

July 1943 witnessed a higher rate of sinkings. Some U-boats ventured back into the North Atlantic, where 18 merchant ships totalling about 123,000 tons were lost, as well as 11 totalling 80,000 tons in the South Atlantic. But the U-boats lost heavily, with the destruction of 33 providing another major defeat for Dönitz. Twelve of these were sunk in the Bay of Biscay, where the tactics of sailing in groups was not working in his favour. When one of the U-boat groups was picked up on the ASV Mark III and then shadowed, the patrolling aircraft called for reinforcements and attacked en masse. In the North Atlantic aircraft from the escort carriers took a heavy toll of the U-boats.

On 2 August 1943 Dönitz reversed his previous decision and ordered his U-boats to cease travelling on the surface through the Bay of Biscay during daylight hours. They were to remain submerged, only surfacing at night to recharge their batteries when necessary. Only two merchant ships totalling 10,000 tons were sunk in the North Atlantic during August, with another two totalling 15,000 tons in the South Atlantic. Although sinkings of U-boats in the Bay of Biscay declined, 20 were destroyed in the Atlantic during the month, primarily from air attack.

At the end of August Dönitz tried another tactic. A total of 22 U-boats and a supporting U-boat tanker hugged the coasts of France and Spain before heading for a new attack in the North Atlantic. Another 6 left from Norway and Germany. Each was fitted with the increased flak armament and its torpedoes included two new acoustic homing versions, to be used against the naval escorts. One U-boat was sunk on 7 September off the Spanish coast by a Leigh Light Wellington, but 27 reached their patrol line to intercept the fast Convoy ON202. Included in the escorts of this convoy was a modified grain carrier, the merchant vessel *Empire MacAlpine*, which was fitted with a flight deck and a hangar and carried four Swordfish of the Fleet Air Arm. This was the first of nineteen such vessels, known as merchant aircraft carriers or MAC-ships. Unlike the American-built escort carriers commissioned into the Royal Navy, they remained merchant vessels and could carry only three or four Swordfish, but they provided additional air cover for the convoys.

Another U-boat attacking Convoy ON202 was sunk on 19 September by a Liberator of the RCAF from Newfoundland. However, on the following day the frigate HMS *Lagan*, escorting Convoy ON202, was badly damaged by a homing torpedo. Three merchant vessels were then torpedoed and sunk. The destroyer HMCS *St Croix* was the next to be hit by one of these torpedoes, sinking an hour later. But a Liberator of 120 Squadron destroyed another of the U-boats, ironically by dropping a homing torpedo. Later in the day the corvette HMS *Polyanthus* was sunk by another homing torpedo. Fog then enveloped the convoy but two days later it was the turn of the frigate HMS *Itchen*, which went down with the survivors of HMCS *St Croix*. Swordfish from the *Empire MacAlpine* and Liberators from Iceland kept many of the U-boats submerged, but the final losses for the convoy were 3 Royal Navy escorts and 6 merchant ships.

Another 2 merchant ships were lost in the North Atlantic during September, bringing the final tally to 8, totalling 44,000 tons, while 3 more, totalling 11,000 tons, were sunk in the South Atlantic. In all, 4 U-boats were destroyed, all by air attack. Dönitz believed that more merchant ships had been sunk and was able to claim a minor victory.

By this time Italy had surrendered to the Allies and turned against her former partner, restricting the movement of U-boats in the Mediterranean, although the Wehrmacht continued to hold much of the country. Seven U-boats were ordered to pass through the Straits of Gibraltar to go to the aid of the German forces, but not all were successful. Dönitz ordered that in future all U-boats making this attempt were to be fitted with the new 'Naxos' receiver, although in tests this had proved less than reliable. October was another dreadful month for him, with 24 U-boats destroyed in return for 12 merchant ships totalling 56,000 tons sunk in the North Atlantic and one of 5,000 tons in the South Atlantic. In this month the RAF was able to provide further coverage of the 'Atlantic Gap' by opening the airfield of Lagens in the Azores, by arrangement with the Portuguese government.

The last two months of the year brought no remission for the U-boats, increasingly hunted by the ever-growing and increasingly effective Allied aircraft. They sank 6 merchant ships in the North Atlantic in November, totalling 23,000 tons, plus one of 4,500 tons in the South Atlantic, for the loss of 18 of their number. December was less active, with 7 merchant ships totalling 48,000 tons sunk in the North Atlantic and none in the South Atlantic, for the destruction of 5 more U-boats. Almost all convoys were now crossing the Atlantic unscathed.

The first of the merchant aircraft carriers (MAC-ships) was the MV *Empire MacAlpine* of 7,950 tons, shown here. This was a converted grain carrier, fitted with a flight deck and a hangar as well one 4-inch, two 20-mm Bofors and four 20-mm anti-aircraft guns. Such vessels sailed in the main body of the convoy, carrying not only cargo but Swordfish to tackle U-boats with depth-charges or rockets. This MAC-ship was commissioned on 14 April 1943 and made her first trip on 29 May 1943 from Halifax in Nova Scotia with the westbound convoy ON59, carrying four Swordfish of the Fleet Air Arm's 836 Squadron.

Maritime Photo Library

An unhappy year for the Kriegsmarine culminated on 26 December with the sinking of the battleship *Scharnhorst* off the North Cape of Norway by a British battle squadron, after she had attempted to intercept a Russian convoy. Two days later a German destroyer and two torpedo-boats were sunk in the Bay of Biscay by two British cruisers, while setting out to escort the inward-bound blockade runner *Alsterufer* which, unknown to them, had already been sunk by a Liberator of Coastal Command. Although outgunned by the German force of 11 destroyers or torpedo-boats, the Royal Navy cruisers fought a successful battle.

Great dark clouds were gathering round Germany, with her forces already in retreat on the Eastern Front. But Dönitz remained determined. German technology had devised a new form of U-boat which might yet turn the tables on his enemies.

The Type VIIC *U-441*, under the command of Kapitänleutnant Klaus Hartmann, undergoing trials in early 1942 after being built by Shifau Werft of Danzig. It was lost with all hands around 18 June 1944 in the Bay of Biscay, almost certainly by air attack, but the exact circumstances are unclear.

U-Boot-Archiv, Cuxhaven-Altenbruch

A Junkers Ju88C-6 long-range fighter with unusual camouflage, on the strength of III./Zerstörergeschwader 1 based at Bordeaux-Mérignac, escorting a U-boat in January 1944. Powered by two Junkers Jumo J-1 or J-2 engines, it had a maximum speed of about 310mph at average weight and a range without auxiliary tanks of about 1,800 miles. The forward-firing armament usually consisted of two machine-guns and a cannon in the nose plus two machine-guns in a gondola underneath. For defensive purposes there were two machine-guns facing backwards in the dorsal canopy and another in the gondola. This was a formidable fighter which was often more than a match for Coastal Command aircraft.

Jean-Louis Roba collection

Kameraden by Mark Postlethwaite GAvA
Junkers Ju88C-6s of 5./Kampfgeschwader 40 escorting a Type VIIC U-boat in the Bay of Biscay.

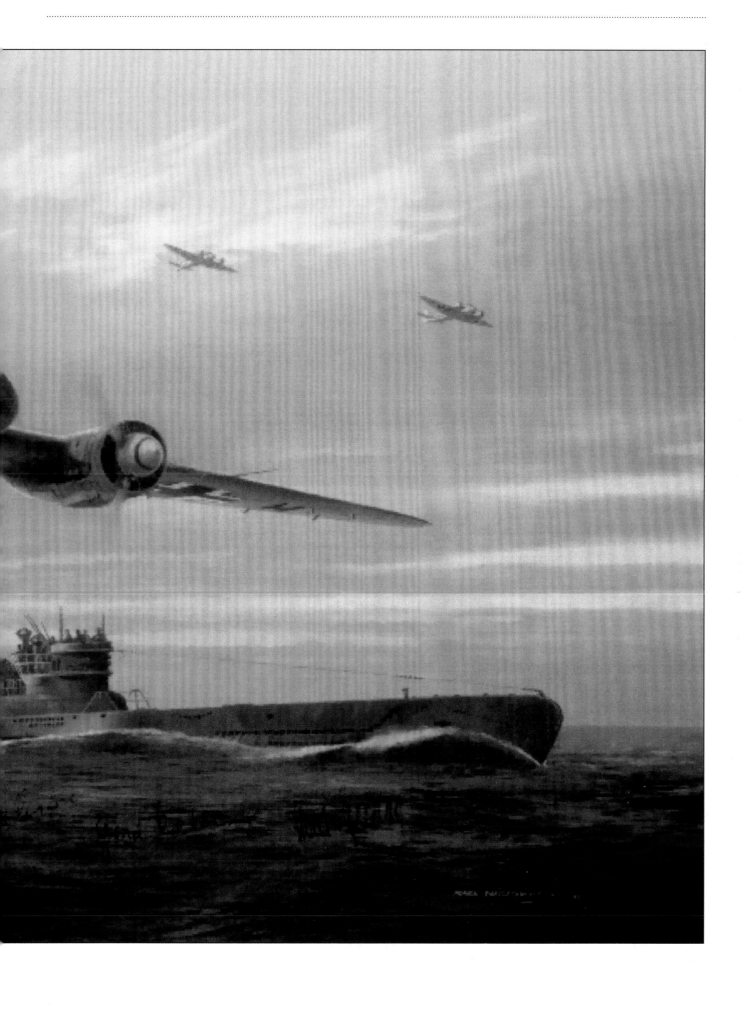

The Type VIIC U-boat *U-960* practising with its 88-mm gun during trials in the Baltic Sea in February 1943.

Fregattenkapitän a.D. Günther Heinrich

The Type VIIC *U-960* surfacing in the Baltic Sea during a training exercise in March 1943, before leaving on its first war cruise. It was commissioned on 28 January 1943. The main periscope is partly extended.

Fregattenkapitän a.D. Günther Heinrich

A Hudson of 200 Squadron flying from one of its airfields in The Gambia in March 1943. At this time the squadron was engaged on anti-submarine patrols and convoy escorts.

Imperial War Museum TR750

HMS *Tracker*, of 11,420 tons displacement, formerly the USS *Mormacmail* launched on 7 March 1942, was one of the escort carriers employed in the North Atlantic and on convoys to North Russia. Such vessels were converted from Merchant Navy hulls in US shipyards. This carrier was equipped with 9 Swordfish and 6 Seafires of 816 Squadron up to the end of 1943, as shown here, and then with 12 Avengers and 7 Wildcats of 846 Squadron to June 1944.

Bruce Robertson collection

One of the *Bogue* class escort carriers built in America but commissioned by the Royal Navy. They normally carried Seafires and Avengers, such as the Avengers on the deck of this vessel.

Bruce Robertson collection

A Grumman Avenger making a practice drop with a Mark 13 torpedo.

Bruce Robertson collection

The single-seat Vought F4U-1 Corsair earned a reputation as the best fighter of the US Navy in the Second World War, after its entry into squadron service in September 1942. Fitted with a Pratt & Whitney R-2800-8 Double Wasp engine of 2,000hp and armed with six 0.50-inch machine-guns, it could achieve a maximum speed of 417mph at about 20,000ft. First employed as a land-based fighter, the F4U-1 was followed by other variants which served on US and Royal Navy escort carriers. Production of the 'gull-wing' Corsair continued for eleven years. It was the last piston-engined fighter to serve in the US forces.

Bruce Robertson collection

The Type IXC *U-161* commanded by Kapitänleutnant Albrecht Achilles, photographed at the end of March 1943 from the blockade runner *Pietro Orseolo*, during the last part of her homeward run from Kobe in Japan to Le Verdon in France. This was an ocean-going type of U-boat. The large 105-mm deck gun forward of the conning tower had been removed to make way for more flak guns. A new gun platform had been installed, awaiting the replacement guns. The two forward jumping wires indicate that the boat was fitted with a rigid radar array on the front of the conning tower. This U-boat was sunk on 27 September 1943 by depth-charges dropped by a Martin Mariner flying boat of VP-74 Squadron, flown by Lieutenant (Junior Grade) H.B. Paterson of the US Navy.

Jak P. Mallmann Showell collection

A Lockheed Hudson fitted with eight rails and rockets in April 1943 at the Aeroplane & Armament Experimental Establishment at Boscombe Down in Wiltshire, for employment on anti-shipping work with Coastal Command. Hudsons were involved in the destruction or surrender of twenty-four U-boats.

Bruce Robertson collection

Bletchley House in Buckinghamshire, photographed in June 2001. It was taken over in 1938 by the Government Code and Cypher School, headed by Commander Alistair Denniston RN of the Foreign Office. The number of staff, all sworn to absolute secrecy, grew from 200 in 1939 to about 7,000 by the end of the war. It is now a museum open to the public.

Author's collection

Hut 4 at Bletchley Park, where cryptanalysts worked on breaking the Enigma codes of the Kriegsmarine.

Author's collection

A German Enigma machine at Bletchley Park, one of 40,000 used by the Wehrmacht during the Second World War. This example has only three rotor wheels. The first version of the Enigma machine was made by a German, Arthur Scherbius, in the 1920s for commercial purposes. It was adopted by the Wehrmacht in the 1930s, and they produced their own portable and battery-operated version.

Author's collection

A reconstructed bombe unit, standing about 6ft high, at Bletchley Park. These electro-mechanical machines were used to decrypt the coded Enigma messages brought to the Government Code and Cypher School from the 'Y' listening stations. The name 'bombe' was first given by Polish code-breakers to their version of a similar machine shortly before the war. The German Enigma codes were broken at Bletchley Park by such machines from 1 August 1940. Over 200 of them were in use by 1944, at Bletchley Park and other secret locations in North Buckinghamshire.

Author's collection

The U-boat yards at Wilhelmshaven were attacked by the US Eighth Air Force on 22 March 1943, when 76 Flying Fortresses and 26 B-24 Liberators were dispatched. They dropped 448 general-purpose bombs of 1,000lb, losing three aircraft during the operation. This B-17 was photographed over the outskirts of the naval base.

Author's collection

The Type VIIC *U-266*, commanded by Kapitänleutnant Ralf von Jesson, was on the surface about 350 miles south-west of Land's End on 15 May 1943 when it was picked up by radar in Halifax II serial HR746 of 58 Squadron, flown from St Eval in Cornwall by the commanding officer, Wing Commander Wilfred E. Oulton. Depth-charges straddled the U-boat, as shown in this photograph by an F24 camera mounted vertically with exposures taken rearward through a mirror. The bows lifted out of the water before the boat sank, leaving no survivors.

Author's collection

The US Eighth Air Force dispatched 38 B-17 Flying Fortresses on 29 May 1943 to attack the U-boat base at La Pallice in France. They dropped almost 200 tons of bombs and caused considerable destruction to the dock area, without losing any aircraft.

Author's collection

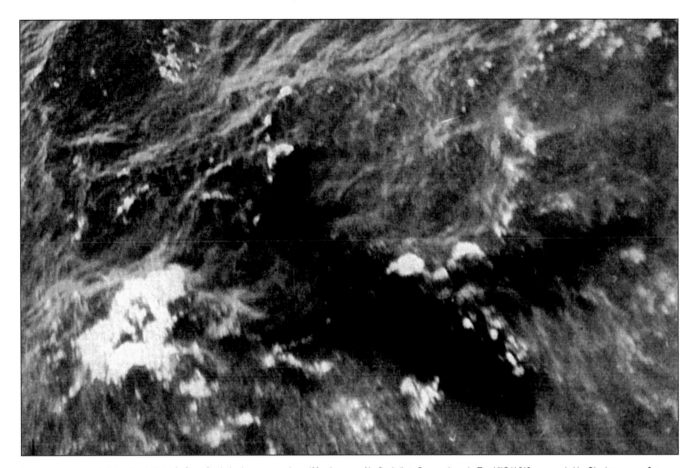

This unusual photograph shows the shadow of a Short Sunderland over a spot about 400 miles west of La Rochelle in France where the Type VIIC *U-563*, commanded by Oberleutnant zur See Gustav Borchardt, was sunk on 31 May 1943. This U-boat was first spotted from Halifax II serial HR774 of 58 Squadron flown from St Eval in Cornwall by the commanding officer, Wing Commander Wilfred E. Oulton. His attack with depth-charges and machine-guns caused damage. It was followed by an attack by another Halifax II, serial DT636, flown by Pilot Officer E.L. Hartley, whose depth-charges fell short. Then Sunderland serial DV969 of 10 (RAAF) Squadron arrived from Mount Batten, flown by Flight Lieutenant M.S. Mainprize, and two more sticks of depth-charges caused the U-boat to begin sinking. Finally Sunderland serial DD838 of 228 Squadron arrived from Pembroke Dock, flown by Flying Officer W.M. French, who delivered the *coup de grâce*.

Author's collection

A Bristol Beaufighter firing rockets fitted with 25lb solid-shot warheads. On 1 June 1943 Flying Officer Mark C. Bateman in Beaufighter VIC serial T5258 of 236 Squadron from Predannack in Cornwall sank with rockets the Type VIIC *U-418*, commanded by Oberleutnant zur See Gerhard Lange, about 350 miles south-west of Land's End. The U-boat had left Kiel on 24 April and was heading towards Brest on its homeward run. There were no survivors.

Author's collection

The Type VIIC *U-97* entering port on 5 June 1943, while in the Mediterranean under the command of Kapitänleutnant Hans-Georg Trox. The U-boat was commissioned on 28 September 1940 and made thirteen war cruises, during which it sank 14 ships, including 6 in the Mediterranean. It was sunk on 16 June 1943 by Hudson IIIA serial FH311 of 459 (RAAF) Squadron based at Nicosia in Cyprus but operating from Lydda in Palestine under the captaincy of Flight Sergeant David T. Barnard. Four depth-charges were dropped. One of these scored a direct hit and the explosion severely damaged the Hudson, which returned to base. The U-boat sank and left men in the water, but twenty-one survivors were picked up by ships.

U-Boot-Archiv, Cuxhaven-Altenbruch

This Type IXD U-boat, *U-200*, left Kiel on 12 June 1943 on its first war cruise in the Atlantic, commanded by Kapitänleutnant Heinrich Schonder. It was spotted twelve days later about 350 miles south of Iceland by Liberator I serial AM929 of 120 Squadron, flown on convoy patrol from Reykjavik by an Australian, Flight Lieutenant A.W. Fraser. The gunners on both the U-boat and the Liberator opened fire, and four depth-charges were dropped. Survivors and wreckage were seen in the water but the Liberator was damaged and the flight engineer wounded. Fraser was forced to return to Reykjavik, where he made a difficult but skilful landing.

Author's collection

Leigh Lights were first used by Liberator Vs of 53 Squadron in June 1943, operating over the Bay of Biscay. This photograph was taken at St Eval in 1943, and shows a nacelle-type Leigh Light under the starboard wing. The ancient church of St Eval is on the left of the photograph. This was recently reconsecrated as an RAF church and contains a Book of Remembrance for the RAF and USNAF personnel lost while operating from the station.

Author's collection

The escort carrier HMS *Activity*, of 11,800 tons displacement, was originally laid down in Britain as the MV *Telemachus* and was completed in October 1942. The anti-aircraft armament consisted of two 4-inch guns and twenty-four 20-mm cannon. She was capable of 18 knots and could carry eleven aircraft, such as the anti-submarine Swordfish and the two Martlets in this photograph. She operated with convoys in the North Atlantic and to North Russia.

Oscar Parkes Society

The Modified Flower class corvette HMS *Willowherb*, of 980 tons displacement and capable of 16.5 knots, was built in Canada. She was armed with a 4-inch gun on the forecastle plus several 20-mm Oerlikons on the bridge. This class was also fitted with a Hedgehog mortar, not visible here. There was a Type 272 radar on the bridge and HF/DF in front of the bridge. The photograph was taken in 1943.

Maritime Photo Library

This ocean-going Type IXC, *U-535*, under the command of Kapitänleutnant Helmut Ellmenreich, left Kiel on 25 May 1943 for a war cruise to the Azores. It was attacked about 250 miles south of Iceland on 8 June by a Hudson III of 269 Squadron, flown from Reykjavik by Sergeant R.B. Couchman. Four depth-charges were dropped, causing the U-boat to lose oil, as shown here, but it managed to reach France for repairs. It was sunk on 5 July 1943 in the Bay of Biscay by Liberator V serial BZ751 of 53 Squadron, flown from St Eval by Flight Sergeant W. Anderson of the RNZAF. There were no survivors.

Author's collection

On 4 July 1943 83 B-17 Flying Fortresses of the US Eighth Air Force were dispatched to bomb the lock-gates at La Pallice, as part of the Battle of the Atlantic. Most of the 275 general-purpose bombs of 1,000lb fell accurately in the target area. In addition to other damage, a Sperrbrecher (heavily armed flak-ship and mine-exploding vessel) received a direct hit. One aircraft failed to return.

Author's collection

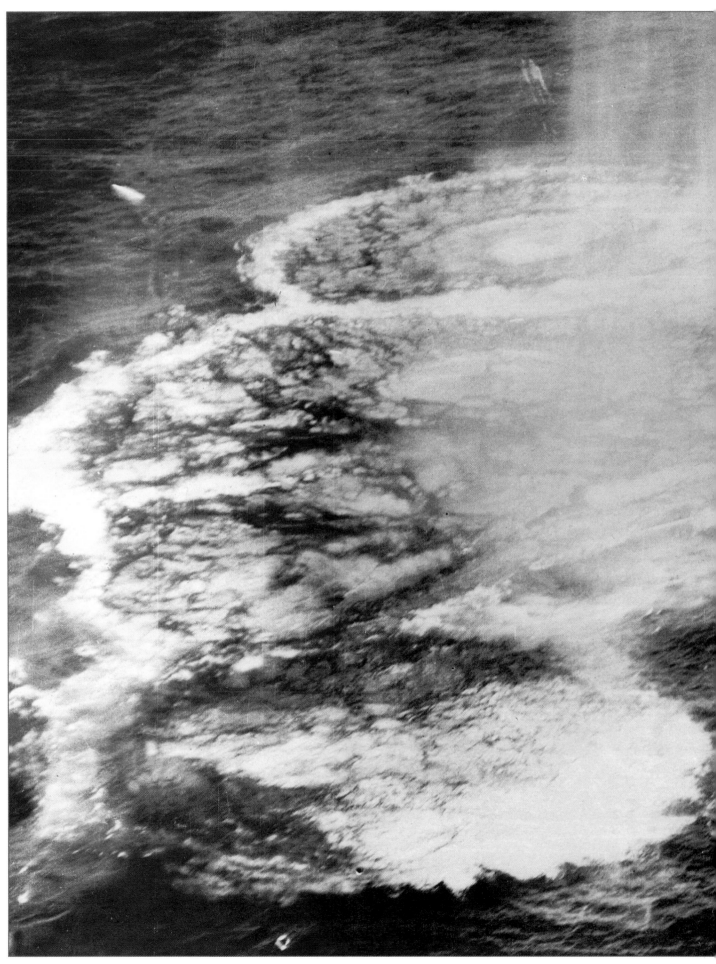

This Type IXD U-boat, *U-106*, under the command of Oberleutnant zur See Wolfdietrich Damerow, was depth-charged in the Bay of Biscay in the morning of 2 August 1943 by Wellington XII serial HF127 of 407 (RCAF) Squadron flown from Chivenor in North Devon by the commanding officer, Wing Commander J.C. Archer. It survived this attack but was sunk about 11 hours later by Sunderland III serial JM708 flown by Flying Officer R.D. Hanbury of 228 Squadron and Sunderland III serial DV968 flown by Flight Lieutenant I.A.F. Clark of 461 (RAAF) Squadron, both based at Pembroke Dock. The Royal Navy picked up thirty-seven survivors.

Author's collection

For Valour by Charles J. Thompson GAvA, ASAA, GMA, EAA

At 09.45 hours on 11 August 1943 Consolidated Liberator V of 200 Squadron, flown from Yundum in The Gambia by Flying Officer Lloyd A. Trigg, attacked the Type VIIC *U-468* on the surface about 240 miles south-west of Dakar. Fire from the U-boat set the Liberator on fire but Trigg continued his attack and dropped his depth-charges before crashing in the sea, killing all crew members. The U-boat sank and the only sailors to survive were the commander Oberleutnant zur See Clemens Schamong and six of his crew, who managed to inflate the Liberator's dinghy, which had been thrown clear. They were spotted the next day by a Sunderland of 204 Squadron from Bathurst and picked up by the corvette HMS *Clarkia*. After Schamong described the Liberator's attack to his captors, Trigg was awarded a posthumous Victoria Cross.

Vaddi Schultze, a crew member of the Type VIIB *U-48*, trying out a new type of machine-gun. This U-boat was decommissioned on 25 September 1943 at Neustadt in Germany, after sinking fifty-nine Allied vessels, and became an instructional boat.

Jak P. Mallmann Showell collection

Lookouts on the Type XIV *U-461*, a large supply boat with workroom facilities intended to allow U-boat flotillas to operate in distant waters in combination with pocket battleships. It was sunk north-west of Spain on 30 July 1943, under the command of Korvettenkapitän Wolf-Harro Stiebler, by Sunderland III serial W6077 of 461 (RAAF) Squadron, flown from Pembroke Dock by Flight Lieutenant Dudley Marrows. Three surfaced U-boats, a Halifax and a US Liberator were involved in the action. Marrows dropped seven depth-charges and his Sunderland was hit by flak. Nevertheless the crew dropped a dinghy to German sailors struggling in the water, 53 of whom died and 15 were rescued. Stiebler was one of the survivors. He met Marrows many years later during a visit to Australia, in far more congenial circumstances.

U-Boot-Archiv, Cuxhaven-Altenbruch

The Fairey Firefly F1 was a two-seat carrier-borne aircraft employed as a fighter-bomber and for reconnaissance by the Fleet Air Arm. It was powered by a Rolls-Royce Griffon IIB engine of 1,730hp and armed with four 20-mm cannon. It first went into service with 1770 Squadron in October 1943.

Author's collection

The Type VIIC *U-960* near Narvik in August 1943, painted white as part of the Arctic Flotilla. A depot ship is in the background. The U-boat left Bergen on 12 August 1943 for its first war cruise.

Fregattenkapitän a.D. Günther Heinrich

The Type VIIC *U-960* at Narvik in September 1943, after returning from its war cruise in the western Siberian Sea. Two 20-mm cannon can be seen aft of the conning tower. On the front of the conning tower is a plaque showing an eagle with a trident in its claws; this was a gift from the 'Friends of the Fleet' in Potsdam, who adopted this boat. An anti-torpedo boom and net are in the background.

Fregattenkapitän a.D. Günther Heinrich

The port area of La Pallice was attacked once more by the US Eighth Air Force, on 16 September 1943, when 44 B-17 Flying Fortresses were dispatched. One Fortress was shot down and six others damaged, but the bombing was effective. Bombs fell in the U-boat locks at 'A' and the pens at 'B', both in the rectangle. Another salvo fell on the dispersal area of an airfield, as circled.

Author's collection

An air reconnaissance photograph of the damaged
Tirpitz, together with other German warships, in
Altenfjord after the attack by two four-man midget
submarines of the Royal Navy, known as X-craft, on
22 September 1943. The battleship has the repair ship
Neumark alongside her and is still moored behind
torpedo nets.

Author's collection

Bridging the Gap by Charles J. Thompson GAvA, ASAA, GMA, EAA

A Liberator VI of 220 Squadron, fitted with a retractable radome under the fuselage and a Leigh Light under the starboard wing, over an Allied convoy in mid-Atlantic. The squadron moved to Lagens in the Azores in October 1943 to help close the 'Atlantic Gap', where U-boats had been able to operate safely outside the range of land-based aircraft. The squadron was equipped with Fortresses for over a year, but transferred on to Liberators in December 1944.

The Type IXC *U-540*, commanded by Kapitänleutnant
Lorenz Kasch, was sunk after attacks by two aircraft
from Iceland in the early evening of 17 October 1943,
about 450 miles south-west of Reykjavik. The first was
Liberator V serial BZ712 of 59 Squadron, flown by
Flight Lieutenant E. Knowles on his homeward run to
Meeks Field, who dropped a stick of four depth-
charges, followed by another stick of two. Then
Liberator I serial AM929 of 120 Squadron, also
homeward bound to Reykjavik with Warrant Officer
B. W. Turnbull at the controls, dropped two more
sticks of depth-charges. The U-boat, which had left
Bergen on 4 October, went down leaving about thirty
men in the water. None survived.

Author's collection

Boeing Flying Fortress IIAs of Coastal Command's 206 and 220 Squadrons were sent to Lagens in the Azores during October 1943, after the Portuguese government granted facilities in the islands to the Allies. The Fortresses were then able to help close the 'Atlantic Gap', where U-boats had formerly been able to operate with little danger from aircraft.

Author's collection

A Flying Fortress IIA of Coastal Command taking off from Lagens in the Azores, leaving a trail of dust.

Author's collection

CHAPTER SIX

TWILIGHT OF
THE U-BOATS

Despite his heavy losses in 1943, Dönitz was still able to command 168 operational U-boats in January 1944, with the huge total of 268 more undergoing training and trials. There was still no shortage of volunteers for training in the U-boat arm, even though these men must have known that it was the most dangerous branch of the German armed forces. Doubtless many were impressed by the propaganda photographs of U-boat men in action and exaggerated accounts of their achievements. These omitted the harsh realities of short and unpleasant lives at sea. A few had volunteered for other branches of the Kriegsmarine but were transferred without their consent. Of course, all required lengthy training, beginning with military discipline and then learning a specialised trade. Training on new U-boats was carried out mainly in the Baltic Sea, where the men were formed into crews. Meanwhile the number of experienced commanders had diminished considerably, because of the huge losses sustained in the previous years.

Most of the fighting men in Germany at this time must have been aware that the Wehrmacht was suffering severe reverses and that their cities were being systematically destroyed from the air, but they were buoyed up by Hitler's assurances that 'wonder weapons' were on the way and would reverse their fortunes. Grossadmiral Dönitz pinned his hopes on a new generation of U-boats which German technology had designed and which were already in production.

The ideal was a U-boat that could remain fully submerged throughout its war cruise, and indeed this was technically possible. Professor Hellmuth Walter had been working on such a U-boat for several years, in collaboration with Germania Werft in Kiel. It was powered by a gas turbine driven by a new fuel of highly concentrated hydrogen peroxide which released its own oxygen and thus did not depend on an external supply. Experiments with a Type V boat fitted with such an engine had demonstrated that a speed of over 20 knots could be achieved while submerged. The boat was thus faster than many escort vessels of the Royal Navy on the surface. However, this 'Walter boat' had several drawbacks. Huge quantities of concentrated hydrogen peroxide (called perhydrol) were required and there were no production facilities in Germany or occupied Europe. This fuel was also highly unstable and dangerous. Moreover, if the Walter boats were built in quantity to replace the conventional U-boats, total production would be halved.

The Type XXI was a large ocean-going U-boat designed to replace the Type VIIC. It had a double hull, giving it almost treble the battery space of the conventional U-boat, and was known as an 'electro-boat'. It was also fitted with a snorkel breathing tube. The streamlined shape and greater power gave it an underwater speed of over 16 knots, higher than some Allied escort vessels on the surface. In all, some 300 such boats were ordered, to be built in sections by factories inland and then assembled at Hamburg, Bremen and Danzig. The first was ready for service in January 1945, but the few which were finally launched arrived too late to affect the outcome of the Battle of the Atlantic. Tugs are accompanying the Type XXI electro-boat in this photograph.

Jak P. Mallmann Showell collection

A compromise was required and this was found in the form of the electro-boats. The Walter boat had been designed with two large and streamlined pressure hulls, one on top of the other in the form of a figure eight. The upper hull contained the turbine plus the usual controls and facilities of a U-boat, while the lower hull was simply a huge fuel tank. An engineer on the Walter boat, Heinrich Heep, had suggested in March 1943 that this double hull could be used to treble the battery capacity of the electric motors fitted to the conventional U-boats, while retaining the existing diesel engines. If such a large ocean-going U-boat was produced, it was calculated that it would achieve a submerged speed of 16 knots, about 10 knots faster than conventional U-boats. Moreover, the improved pressure hull would enable the boat to dive to greater depths.

This idea seemed a godsend to Dönitz, who saw the chance of regaining the initiative in the Battle of the Atlantic. The new ocean-going boat was designated the Type XXI, to replace the ubiquitous Type VIIC. A smaller version was also designed, the Type XXIII, for operations in British coastal waters. Dr Albert Speer estimated that his Department of Military Armament could produce about twenty of the Type XXI per month. Both this and the smaller Type XXIII were ordered in bulk. To minimise the effect of Allied bombing they were to be built in dispersed factories inland, each manufacturing different parts, and then assembled in coastal or riverside yards. The method should have resulted in a great improvement in output.

Other weapons were more readily available. These were the midget submarines, which could carry two torpedoes slung underneath them but had limited range. The two-man version was the Seehund (Seal), while there were two one-man versions, the Biber (Beaver) and the Molch (Salamander). These operated in the southern end of the North Sea and were to have very little success, despite the fanatical bravery of the crews. They accounted for a few of the sinkings in the inshore campaign, as did the Schnellboote (fast motor torpedo-boats).

Meanwhile the conventional operational U-boats, mainly the Type VIIC and the Type IXC, were compelled to soldier on and attempt to sink Allied ships in the North Atlantic and other waters. There was a prospect that their defence against air and surface attack could be improved by the installation of a device proposed for the original Walter boat. This was an extensible air tube known as a Schnorkel (snorkel), which would enable them to draw in air when travelling just below the surface of the sea, while under power from their diesel engines. There was nothing new in this design, which had been proposed for submarines of the Royal Netherlands Navy as early as 1933, and subsequently utilised in nine of them. Two German engineers, Heinrich Heep and Ulrich Gabler, devised a snorkel suitable for the existing U-boats. This was a fairly simple rigid tube, with a spherical ball valve to prevent the sea from entering it, which could be extended and retracted like a periscope. After tests in the Baltic, arrangements were made in the winter of 1943/4 to begin fitting these snorkels to some front-line U-boats.

The grim war in the North Atlantic continued, but on a much reduced scale. Only 5 merchant ships totalling 36,000 tons were sunk in the North Atlantic during January 1944, plus 3 totalling 11,500 tons in the South Atlantic, at the cost of 13 U-boats destroyed. The U-boats in the Mediterranean and the Indian Ocean were sinking far more ships than those in the Atlantic, and at a much lower cost.

February 1944 was even worse for the U-boat arm, with only 2 merchant vessels totalling 12,500 tons sunk in the North Atlantic and none in the South Atlantic, while 14 U-boats were destroyed. Among those sunk was the Type VIIC *U-264*, the first to be fitted with the new snorkel. On 19 February it had fallen victim to the sloops HMS *Starling* and HMS *Woodpecker*, while attempting to attack Convoy ON224 west-south-west of Ireland. Although fifty-one of the crew were rescued by the Royal Navy, they were unable to report to Dönitz on the performance of the snorkel.

Then came March 1944, with 7 merchant ships totalling 37,000 tons sunk in the North Atlantic plus another of 4,600 tons in the South Atlantic, while 14 more U-boats were destroyed. The second U-boat fitted with the snorkel, the Type VIIC *U-575*, was sunk on 13 March while off the Azores by aircraft from the carrier USS *Bogue*. However its commander, Oberleutnant Wolfgang Boehmer, had been able beforehand to radio a report on the snorkel to Dönitz. He stated that it was impractical to use the device when being hunted by surface vessels because the noise of the diesel engines drowned the pings of the hydrophones warning him of their approach.

German propaganda could not resist making references to forthcoming new and powerful U-boats. The British were also aware from Enigma and air reconnaissance evidence that construction of the older U-boats was diminishing in favour of newer types of boat. Their suspicions were confirmed on 19 April 1944 when a Mosquito of 540 (PR) Squadron brought back pictures of an ocean-going Type XXI on a slipway at Danzig. This was the first of its kind, *U-3501*, but its completion and that of the coastal electro-boats was being seriously

A bomb-proof factory for the assembly of Type XXIIB
'Seehund' midget submarines. These two-man craft
had a displacement of 15 tons submerged and could
carry two torpedoes, for use mainly in coastal waters.
About 150 were built, production being severely
curtailed by Allied bombing.

Author's collection

delayed. Allied bombing had destroyed much of the factory producing their electric motors, and there were insufficient skilled workers able to repair the damage. Dönitz had hoped that the new electro-boats would be operational in the late summer of 1944, but already the programme was being set back.

The conventional U-boats did not succeed in sinking any ships in the North Atlantic during May 1944 but they accounted for three totalling 17,000 tons in the South Atlantic. Despite their lack of success in these waters, six U-boats were sunk, while others were lost in the North Sea and the Mediterranean. One which returned to St Nazaire on 19 May after a fruitless war cruise in the North Atlantic was the Type VIIC *U-667*. The commander, Kapitänleutnant Karl-Heinz Lange, reported enthusiastically on his experience with the snorkel. He stated that he had remained submerged for nine days without detection and that the batteries could be recharged sufficiently within 3 hours while running on the diesel engines. This report was enough to encourage the U-boat arm to fit snorkels to all U-boats under construction or already in operation, although this placed an additional burden on the overstretched ship-building industry.

There remained certain problems with the snorkel, however, which were not fully overcome. Waves in heavy seas could cause the head-valve to close, so that the diesel engines sucked up the air in the interior of the U-boat, with results that were potentially dangerous. Moreover there was no adequate method of waste disposal in these older U-boats, for it was normally jettisoned. Thus long periods submerged caused the interior to become fouled, from rotting food waste and the nauseating stink from overflowing excrement in the heads.

The strength of Allied naval and air escorts was growing continually. Captain F.J. Walker continued his legendary career as one of the Royal Navy's escort commanders, updating and perfecting a method which was apparently simple but required considerable training. He called it 'Operation Plaster', and it depended on a strong escort force with a large supply of depth-charges.

The U-boat was stalked when an Asdic contact was made, often by three escort vessels in line abreast. Patterns of depth-charges set to explode between 500 and 700ft were dropped in a pattern along its course, giving the commander little chance of evasive action. Walker's 2nd Escort Group sank six U-boats in the Western Approaches during a cruise of 27 days from 31 January 1944. But then, after three years of intensive war in the Atlantic during which he never seemed to tire, this commander died of a stroke on 9 July 1944 and was buried at sea.

Another device which came into service in the spring of 1944 was a replacement for the Hedgehog bomb-throwing mortar. Named the 'Squid', it was much heavier than its predecessor and consisted of three mortars, each of which projected a charge of 350lb up to 700 yards ahead of a ship. It was too heavy for the corvettes but could be fitted to destroyers, sloops and frigates. The first U-boat to be sunk with this weapon was the Type VIIC *U-333*, on 31 July 1944 when west-south-west of the Scillies. This hitherto successful U-boat succumbed to the sloop HMS *Starling* and the new frigate HMS *Loch Killin*, and was lost with all hands.

A much higher proportion of U-boats was being destroyed by air attack, either from land-based or carrier-borne aircraft. The escort carriers of the Royal Navy and the US Navy dominated the central regions of the North Atlantic. The strength of the Fleet Air Arm had grown to 513 fighters or fighter-bombers and 479 strike aircraft by April 1944, although many of these were employed on carriers for the Arctic convoys or were engaged in more distant waters. Coastal Command contributed to the anti-submarine war 2 squadrons of Catalinas, 2 of

The most famous of the Royal Navy's escort leaders, Captain F.J. 'Johnny' Walker, CB, DSO***, DSC**, photographed when a Commander on the bridge of his sloop HMS *Starling*. He died on this bridge on 9 July 1944 when he suffered a stroke, after years of intensive service, and was buried at sea.

Author's collection

The sloop HMS *Starling*, of 1,350 tons displacement and armed with six 4-inch guns, was modified from the *Black Swan* class. She appears to be fitted with a Type 272 'surface search' radar and a Type 285 'air warning' radar. Under Commander F.J. Walker, she succeeded in sinking or participated in the sinking of no fewer than 13 U-boats. According to the available records, these were the Type XB *U-119*, the Type VIICs *U-202, U-226, U-238, U-264, U-333, U-385, U-473, U-592, U-653, U-734* and *U-961*, and the Type IXC/40 *U-864*.

Author's collection

Halifaxes, 2 of Fortresses, 7 of RAF Liberators (plus 3 USAAF or USNAF Liberators under RAF control), 7 of Sunderlands, 5 of Wellingtons and 3 of Hudsons.

Some of these aircraft were provided with a new device developed by US scientists. This was the magnetic airborne detector, known as MAD. It was based on the magnetometer used by mineralogists to detect deposits underground. A far more sensitive airborne instrument was produced which could pick up the magnetic field of a U-boat, about 10 gammas at 400ft compared with the average of 50,000 gammas for the earth's magnetic field. One problem was that the range was so short that normal bombs could not be dropped, since these travelled forward after release, owing to the transmitted velocity of the aircraft. Thus a special bomb was produced with a rocket in its tail which propelled it backwards to counterbalance this forward velocity. Provided aircraft flew at about 100mph, these 'retrobombs' dropped vertically when the aircraft was directly above the target.

The Catalina could carry twenty-four of these retrobombs, each weighing 35lb. The aircraft were aptly named 'Madcats' by the crews. The first to experience their destructive power had been the Type VIIC *U-761*, which attempted to pass through the Straits of Gibraltar on 24 February 1944. It was located by the MAD apparatus installed in two Madcats of the US Navy's VP63 Squadron, based at Port Lyautey in Morocco. They were supported by a Catalina of the RAF's 202 Squadron from Gibraltar. The retrobombs of the Madcats and the depth-charges of the standard Catalina crippled the U-boat, which was then finished off by the destroyers HMS *Anthony* and HMS *Wishart*. Forty-eight of the crew were picked up to become prisoners.

Another invention which had come into operation was also American. It was named the 'sonobuoy' and consisted of a lightweight cylinder about 6ft long which contained a hydrophone. It was dropped by parachute and on hitting the water, the hydrophone detached itself and descended on a cable. It was powered by batteries with a life of about 4 hours, and transmitted signals to the aircraft. The range at which it could detect submarines varied considerably but could be as much as 3 miles if the U-boat's propellers were rotating at high speed.

Apart from these developments, the Mosquitos of a detachment within 248 Squadron of the RAF's Coastal Command had already been adapted to take a Molins gun which fired 6-pounder explosive shells. These specialised Mosquitos were known as 'Tsetses'. Operating from Cornwall with the other Mosquitos as fighter escorts, they hunted U-boats down the west coast of France. The Type IXB *U-123* had been the first to be hit with one of their shells, on 7 November 1943, while returning from the Trinidad area, but it had been able to reach St Nazaire. The first to be sunk was the Type VIIC *U-976*, in the Charente estuary on 23 March 1944, also returning to St Nazaire. Most of the crew were rescued by their minesweeper escort. Another U-boat, the Type VIIC *U-960*, was hit by one of these Tsetses on 27 March 1944, but in turn it damaged the aircraft with return fire.* Coastal Command was also providing squadrons of Beaufighters which rampaged down this coast, sinking surface vessels of the Kriegsmarine as well as merchant ships.

---

* Long after the war, the author was instrumental in putting the Tsetse pilot, A.H. 'Hilly' Hilliard, and the U-boat commander, Günther 'Heini' Heinrich, in touch with each other. The two men developed a firm friendship.

The de Havilland Mosquito VI fighter-bomber entered service with Coastal Command in December 1943 as an anti-shipping strike aircraft. It was armed with four 20-mm cannon and four 0.303-inch machine-guns, and could carry two 500lb bombs or eight rockets. The cannon in some of these aircraft were removed and replaced with a single Molins anti-tank gun protruding underneath the nose, as shown here. These were known as Mark XIIIs or Tsetses.

Author's collection

The Molins gun protruding at a slightly downwards angle underneath the nose of a Tsetse. It emitted a flame up to 20ft long when first installed and a flash eliminator was fitted (not shown). The use of the gun in testing caused a crack to appear between the barrel and the four machine-guns. This was solved by removing the two outer machine-guns (see cover plate in this photograph) and installing tie rods between the remaining two machine-guns and the bottom part of the nose.

Author's collection

It was apparent to German Intelligence that the Allies would launch an invasion against the 'Western Wall' in the summer of 1944, but the exact location and timing were not known to them. Both sides knew that the heavier German warships could do nothing to hinder these landings. The battleship *Tirpitz* was under repair in Kaafjord after an attack by the Fleet Air Arm on 3 April 1944. The pocket battleships *Admiral von Scheer* and *Lützow* and the heavy cruisers *Admiral Hipper* and *Prinz Eugen* were stationed in the Baltic, as were four remaining light cruisers. They were engaged either in training or in support of the German armies on the Eastern Front. If any attempted to break out into the North Sea, the Royal Navy's Home Fleet was eager to deal with them.

Allied deception plans had worked well and Hitler believed that the landings would be made in the Pas de Calais, where his generals were confident that they would be repulsed. When Allied airborne troops began landing in Normandy in the early hours of 6 June 1944, followed by waves of troops storming the beaches, it was considered to be a diversionary tactic. The truth did not dawn on the generals until the following morning. Three destroyers in the Gironde, the torpedo-boats at Le Havre and the Schnellboote (called E-boats by the RAF) at Cherbourg were ordered to attack the landing craft.

The three destroyers in the Gironde were spotted leaving the estuary and two were damaged on D-Day by Beaufighters of Coastal Command when near Belle Ile. All three put into Brest while repairs were carried out. Four torpedo-boats from Le Havre managed to sink a Norwegian destroyer before escaping back to their port under cover of a smokescreen. On 8 June the three destroyers slipped out of Brest, together with a torpedo-boat, but were engaged by a destroyer flotilla of the Royal Navy which sank one, damaged another which was beached and finished off by the Beaufighters, and sent the other destroyer and the torpedo-boat back into Brest. There were eighteen Schnellboote available to attack the eastern flank of the invasion force. In four nights of operations they managed to sink 5 landing craft, a motor torpedo-boat, a motor gunboat and 3 small merchant ships, as well as damaging other warships. Four of their number were sunk.

Dönitz was on leave with his family in the Black Forest when the invasion began, but he hastened to his U-boat High Command near Berlin, to find that the 36 U-boats available in the Biscay bases and the 22 U-boats in southern Norway had been put on full alert. Another five U-boats from France heading for the North Atlantic had been recalled, while 7 at sea from Norway bound for the Atlantic were to await further orders. Dönitz ordered that every U-boat was to be 'flung into the battle regardless of cost'.

In the event 8 U-boats fitted with snorkels and 9 more without snorkels, all based at Brest, were ordered to move on the surface to the English Channel and attack the western flank of the Allied invasion force. All sailed in the afternoon and evening of D-Day. The commanders were told that every Allied ship was a target and that they were to press home their attacks regardless of any danger to their boats. The other 19 U-boats based at Lorient, St Nazaire and La Pallice were ordered to form a patrol line in the Bay of Biscay, in case the Allies attempted to land somewhere on the Atlantic coast. None of these was fitted with a snorkel.

The relevant Enigma signals, other than those concerning the patrol line in the Bay of Biscay, were intercepted by the British 'Y' service, passed to Bletchley Park and decrypted. By the night of D-Day Beaufighters of Coastal Command had spotted and reported numerous U-boats heading on the surface for the Channel.

The Fairey Barracuda was a three-seat carrier-borne aircraft with folding wings, employed by the Fleet Air Arm from December 1942 as a torpedo-bomber and dive-bomber. The Mark I was powered by a Rolls-Royce Merlin 30 engine of 1,200hp, but the Mark II and Mark III were fitted with a Merlin 32 of 1,640hp. All were armed with a pair of Vickers K guns in the rear cockpit and could carry a torpedo or four depth-charges, or an equivalent weight of bombs. The Mark III was fitted with a radome below the rear fuselage. This photograph shows a Mark II carrying a torpedo.

Courtesy of Aeroplane

During the early morning of 7 June these were subjected to continual attacks from Sunderlands, Wellingtons, Liberators, Halifaxes and Tsetses. Two were sunk and four so badly damaged that they were forced to turn back to Brest, although a Wellington and three Liberators were shot down. Two more were sunk on 8 June and another turned back with damage to Brest. One was sunk on 10 June and another forced to turn back with damage on the following day. Another had to turn back with snorkel trouble. Thus 12 of the original 17 were sunk or damaged and achieved no sinkings.

Meanwhile 4 of the U-boats south of Iceland from Norwegian bases were ordered to head for the Channel, together with the 5 in the Atlantic from France, to reinforce the remaining 5 U-boats from Brest. Of the latter, 3 had put into St Peter Port in Guernsey to recharge their batteries and enable their exhausted crews to rest after sleepless days and nights. Only 2 of the 9 U-boats dispatched to their support managed to penetrate the Allied screens and begin attacks. In the remaining days of the month these 7 U-boats sank one frigate, damaged another, and damaged four American Liberty ships. But 3 more U-boats were sunk in the Channel.

The 19 U-boats forming a patrol line in the Bay of Biscay were also subjected to frequent air attacks. One was sunk and another returned damaged. The other 17 were recalled on 12 June, to shelter in their concrete bunkers rather than risk annihilation in the North Atlantic. There were still 22 operational U-boats in Norway, based at Bergen, Stavanger and Christiansand. These were held in readiness to repel an invasion, for Hitler had been convinced by the Allied deception plans that this was imminent. They were reinforced by 8 from Kiel, and 16 were sent out to form a patrol line against an invasion fleet. Four of these were sunk by RAF air attack.

The disastrous month of June 1944 cost Dönitz 26 U-boats sunk in all theatres, mostly in the Channel or in the Atlantic. Only 2 ships totalling 4,000 tons were sunk in the North Atlantic, plus another of 3,000 tons in the South Atlantic. The existence of the Biscay bases was in peril, as the next few weeks would demonstrate.

By early July German Intelligence had established the pattern of the Allied supply lines across the Channel to Normandy, and the U-boats in France were sent in again. Only those with snorkels were dispatched, all travelling submerged and forbidden to raise their breathing tubes during daylight hours for fear of detection. Conditions within them became foul, but could only be relieved at night. Then they entered waters which were shallow and swarming dangerously with warships. One small freighter was sunk on 5 July but a U-boat was depth-charged and sunk by warships on the same day, and another on the following day. Meanwhile aircraft picked off two more U-boats in the Bay of Biscay. Another U-boat was sunk on 14 July by an RAF mine off Brest. One was sunk in the Channel by warships on 18 July and another three days later. By this time the RAF had sunk 4 more off the Norwegian coasts. An RAF bombing raid on Kiel during the night of 23/24 July accounted for 4 more and 2 others were sunk by warships in the Channel before the month was out. It was another terrible month for Dönitz, who lost 23 U-boats in all waters, and accomplished little. In the North Atlantic only 2 merchant vessels totalling almost 6,000 tons were sunk in July, plus 2 totalling 14,000 tons in the South Atlantic.

Yet the sea war in the Channel continued. Another U-boat was sunk in these waters on 4 August. One succeeded in sinking a Liberty ship on 8 August and a corvette on the same day. In all, 8 U-boats were operating in the Channel by 14 August but one was sunk on the following day. But by this time 5 more U-boats had been sunk in the Bay of Biscay, all but one from the air. The Wehrmacht had lost the Battle of Normandy and strong elements of Lieutenant-General George S. Patten's US Third Army were streaking towards the Brittany ports. On 12 August Lancasters of Bomber Command dropped 12,000lb Tallboy bombs, partially penetrating the roof of the bunker in Brest. All the serviceable U-boats in Brest, Lorient and St Nazaire were ordered to head for La Pallice and Bordeaux, and were hunted by Allied warships and aircraft en route.

By 18 August, three days after American forces landed in the south of France and began to fight their way to the north, Hitler ordered the evacuation of western France, apart from troops who were to form 'fortresses' in the ports of Brest, Lorient, St Nazaire, La Pallice, La Rochelle and an area near Bordeaux. Dönitz ordered 16 of the remaining seaworthy U-boats to head round the north of Scotland for Norwegian ports, while 8 more were to cover them by operating off the Bristol Channel and the North Channel (between Scotland and Ireland) for about 10 days before following them to Norway. In all, 9 U-boats were left behind to be broken up or scuttled. Including these, 36 U-boats were destroyed in August, in all theatres. Only one merchant ship, of almost 6,000 tons, was sunk in the neglected North Atlantic, while none was sunk in the South Atlantic. All the naval vessels of the Kriegsmarine on the Atlantic coast were sunk, mainly by air attack from Beaufighters and Mosquitos of Coastal Command, or were scuttled. Yet Dönitz refused to give up the struggle and exhorted his crews to remain true to the National Socialist State and to fight on fanatically.

Public Record Office: INF 13/216/3

Elsewhere, operations by U-boats also came to an end. Six Type IIB coastal U-boats had been transported in sections from the Baltic to the Black Sea, where they were reassembled to operate in these waters. Some were damaged during Russian air raids on Constanza in Romania and all were blown up or scuttled in September, to avoid being cut off by the advancing Russians. The U-boats which still operated in the Mediterranean were also eliminated during August and September 1944. The last to sail on a war cruise was sunk by destroyers of the Royal Navy on 19 September. The remaining two were destroyed on 24 September during a bombing raid on Salamis in Greece by US Liberators. Although a handful of German-controlled surface vessels was still active in Aegean waters, Allied ships could now sail unimpeded through the Mediterranean and the Suez Canal, while some of their naval escorts were released to fight in other areas.

By this time active U-boat bases were reduced to those in Norway and Germany, apart from a handful in the Far East. The passage to the Atlantic was, of course, far longer from the Norwegian bases than from their former Biscay bunkers, and moreover there were insufficient facilities or shelters in the Norwegian ports to cope with the additional U-boats. The 8 U-boats from the Biscay bases ordered to cover the withdrawal of the other 16 were reinforced by 10 more from Norway, but these achieved very little in September. Only 3 merchant ships were sunk in the North Atlantic, totalling about 16,500 tons, plus 3 more totalling about 21,000 tons in inshore waters. But 21 U-boats were lost in the month, in all theatres of war.

In October 11 U-boats were sent out from Norway to the North Channel, the Bristol Channel and the English Channel, while 4 more were sent to the coasts of Newfoundland and another to Gibraltar. Knowing that the pens at Bergen were being enlarged to accommodate the U-boats from the Biscay bases, RAF Bomber Command mounted a raid on Bergen harbour during the night of 4/5 October. This destroyed 4 U-boats and caused damage to repair yards and other facilities but the bombs failed to penetrate the roofs of the pens. Unhappily, some civilian casualties were caused. Another 10 U-boats were destroyed during the month from various causes, but only 2 merchant ships were sunk. Both were in the inshore waters of Britain and totalled 1,700 tons.

During November 1944 the U-boats sank 3 merchant ships totalling about 8,000 tons in the North Atlantic plus 3 more totalling about 9,000 tons during their 'inshore campaign', but lost 6 of their number in all theatres. The mighty battleship *Tirpitz* received her quietus at Kaafjord on 12 November, removing any threat to the Arctic or Atlantic convoys, when 30 Lancasters of RAF Bomber Command dropped 'Tallboy' bombs which caused her to capsize. Over half of the 1,900 men on board were killed or injured.

But there were disturbing signs that the anti-submarine war was not over. The U-boat commanders had become more adept with their snorkelling procedures and their boats were becoming more difficult to detect. The snorkel provided only a minimum signal for the radar of a searching aircraft. A radar detection device fixed to the snorkel itself provided an early warning of any aircraft, by day or night. U-boats operating in the inshore campaign were also more difficult to detect by Asdic, since rocks and wrecks produced false echoes. Moreover, the U-boats sent fewer signals to headquarters from these waters, so that the Submarine Tracking Room at the Admiralty was less able to determine their positions. These factors combined to enable the U-boats to sink 18 merchant vessels totalling 85,500 tons in inshore waters during December 1944, plus another of 5,500 tons

The effect of a Leigh Light fitted to a Coastal Command Liberator, switched on at night while on the ground. The photograph is dated October 1944.

Author's collection

in the North Atlantic. In return, 15 U-boats were destroyed in all areas, including 2 from the bombing of Hamburg by the US Eighth Air Force and 2 from accidents.

Dönitz began 1945 with 144 operational U-boats plus 246 under training or undergoing trials. Unlike many other Nazi leaders, he seems to have believed that Germany would find the strength and ability to overcome its enemies, in spite of the failure of the Wehrmacht against the Western Allies in the 'Battle of the Bulge' and its steady retreat from the Russians on the Eastern Front. He was devoted to Hitler and convinced he could somehow turn the tide. His own contribution was to be the new electro-boats which were overcoming their teething troubles and nearing entry into the Battle of the Atlantic.

The Allies were well aware of this danger, from both Enigma decrypts and photo-reconnaissance, and were intent on containing it. They knew that 35 ocean-going Type XXIs were working up to operational efficiency and that others were under construction, as were many of the coastal Type XIIIs. Some heavy bombers of the RAF and the USAAF were diverted from their main task of destroying German synthetic oil plants and transportation systems to attacking the assembly yards. A very effective raid took place on 17 January 1945 when the US Eighth Air Force bombed Hamburg, destroying 3 Type XXIs and seriously damaging 9 others.

But such attacks did little to hinder the main flow of electro-boat construction. The first electro-boat to carry out a war cruise was the coastal Type XXIII *U-2324*, which sailed from the Norwegian port of Horten on 29 January. This

Tirpitz – Mission Accomplished by Mark Postlethwaite
GAvA

Avro Lancasters of 617 and 9 Squadrons deliver the
final blow to the huge German battleship *Tirpitz* at
Tromsö in Norway, dropping 12,000lb *Tallboy* bombs
on 12 November 1944.

was mainly a familiarisation exercise but on 18 February the commander fired his armament of two torpedoes at a convoy off Newcastle-on-Tyne. Both missed and the U-boat returned. In addition, 17 conventional U-boats were dispatched during January 1945. Apart from those lost by air bombardment, 11 U-boats were lost in all areas, but 5 merchant ships totalling 29,000 tons were sunk in the North Atlantic, plus 12 totalling 46,500 tons in British inshore waters.

By February 1945 strenuous efforts in the Norwegian bases had resulted in improved facilities, sufficient for 29 U-boats to be dispatched. Among these was another of the coastal Type XXIII, *U-2322*, which left Horten on 6 February. It managed to sink a merchant vessel of 1,300 tons off the east coast of Scotland and returned safely. Meanwhile 12 conventional boats were sent into the English Channel, but by then the Admiralty had swamped the inshore waters with anti-submarine warships. Only 3 survived their cruises, although 4 merchant vessels were sunk. During the month 5 merchant vessels totalling 32,500 tons were sunk in the North Atlantic, plus 19 totalling 48,500 tons in the inshore campaign. But February cost Dönitz 22 U-boats destroyed, including one in a US air raid on Bremen.

Nevertheless, the U-boat arm continued its unequal struggle, dispatching 25 U-boats from Norway during March. The third operational Type XXIII, *U-2321*, was sent out from Horten on 9 March, but returned without having sighted any targets off the east coast of Britain. The other U-boats succeeded in sinking 3 merchant vessels totalling 23,500 tons in the North Atlantic and another of 3,500 tons in the South Atlantic, while 23 ships totalling 83,500 tons were lost in the inshore campaign. In return, 17 U-boats were destroyed in all waters. Some of the aircraft of Coastal Command had been equipped with a new Air to Surface-Vessel radar, the ASV Mark X, which operated on a 3cm wave-band and was more capable of picking up signals from snorkels. This helped to account for some of the sinkings in March. In addition, 13 more U-boats were destroyed during devastating raids on 30 March by the US Eighth Air Force on Bremen, Wilhelmshaven and Hamburg.

April 1945 was a month of despair for the U-boat arm, and even for Dönitz. An additional 32 U-boats were dispatched from Norwegian bases, and 5 merchant vessels totalling 32,000 tons were sunk in the North Atlantic and 14 totalling 49,500 tons in the inshore campaign. Meanwhile, 3 Type XXIIIs operated off the east coast of Britain, sinking one small ship and damaging another. However, 54 U-boats were sunk at sea or as a result of the bombing of German yards by the RAF and the USAAF. Some of these were sunk by the RAF operating in daylight over the Kattegat. As the Russians advanced, U-boats streamed out of the Baltic and were sent to Horten to continue operating from Norway. Several were caught en route by aircraft of Coastal Command and destroyed.

On 30 April 1945 the only ocean-going electro-boat to undertake a war cruise left Bergen. This was the Type XXI *U-2511*, her original cruise having been interrupted by a damaged periscope. This was also the day when Hitler committed suicide, after unexpectedly appointing Grossadmiral Karl Dönitz as his successor. The new German President knew that the military situation was hopeless and that he had to seek an armistice. However, he stalled for a few days, it seems to allow as many troops and civilians as possible to avoid captivity by the Russians and also to enable the scuttling of his remaining surface fleet. An instrument of surrender of the forces in Northern Germany was signed on 4 May 1945 at the headquarters of the British 21st Army Group on Lüneberg Heath. On the same day orders to surrender were transmitted to all U-boats at sea.

Despite this, a total of 218 were scuttled in the Baltic, including many of the electro-boats working up for war cruises.

The final unconditional surrender to all the Allies took place at Rheims in France in the afternoon of 7 May 1945, in the presence of high-ranking commanders from the United States, Britain, Soviet Russia and France. During those few early days of May 1945, 2 Allied merchant vessels totalling 5,500 tons were sunk in the North Atlantic, as well as 2 totalling 4,500 tons in the inshore campaign. But the U-boats were massacred. Some 28 were sunk, all but 6 while en route from German bases to Norway, by aircraft of the RAF's Coastal Command or the 2nd Tactical Air Force. One which escaped was the ocean-going Type XXI electro-boat *U-2511*, which had reached a position north of the Faroes when the commander received the order to surrender. He made a mock attack on a British cruiser and her destroyer escort before returning undetected to Bergen. The Allies had no answer to these boats, which could have cruised from German ports as far as the Pacific and created havoc with Allied shipping in all waters. The danger was narrowly averted by the conquest of Germany before they became operational.

U-boats sank almost 15 million tons of Allied merchant ships during the war, nearly 70 per cent of the total lost from all causes. They also sank 174 Allied warships or auxiliary vessels. The records show that 1,110 U-boats entered service during the Second World War and of these almost 800 were destroyed by Allied attack, including bombing of yards, or other causes. Some were lost for reasons which cannot be determined. Although the exact percentage can never be

This memorial to the airmen lost over the North Sea was erected on the sea front at Cleethorpes in Lincolnshire and unveiled on 25 September 1999. It was sculpted by Pam Taylor and financed under the auspices of the North Coates Beaufighter Strike Wing, which suffered many casualties in its operations over the North Sea during the Second World War.

Author's collection

accurately calculated, it seems that aircraft plus the combined action of aircraft and warships destroyed a greater number of U-boats than warships alone. This percentage varied considerably as the war progressed. Aircraft were less successful in the first three years, but gained ascendancy from late 1942 onwards. Over 30,000 servicemen in the U-boat arm perished during the war, probably more than 65 per cent of those who served in the front-line boats.

Midget submarines made a total of 244 operational sorties but their mines and torpedoes sank only 16 ships totalling about 19,000 tons. Of these submarines, 105 failed to return, a figure which does not justify the expenditure of effort and the sacrifices made by the gallant crews.

There is only one known instance of a war crime committed by U-boat men. This occurred on 13 March 1944 when the commander of the Type IXD2 *U-852*, Kapitänleutnant Heinz Eck, ordered his men to machine-gun and throw grenades at the survivors of the torpedoed Greek ship SS *Peleus*. But three of these survivors escaped death and lived to tell the tale. Eck and two of his men were executed after conviction at a War Crimes Tribunal. On the other hand, there are several accounts of U-boat men helping the survivors of torpedoed ships, giving them food and other supplies, and directing lifeboats to the nearest land.

The tribulations of the war were not yet over for Karl Dönitz. He was arrested on 23 May 1945 and was among the 22 high-ranking Nazis brought before the International Military Tribunal which opened at Nuremberg on 20 November 1945. The Admiralty believed that in his case there was no case to answer and that he had merely been carrying out his patriotic duty, but the Americans considered that someone responsible for the sinking of so many merchant ships, and who had been named as Hitler's successor, should be tried.

In the event Dönitz was arraigned on the first three of the five counts specified by the Tribunal. These were conspiracy to wage war, crimes against peace and crimes against humanity. He was acquitted on the first count but found guilty on the other two and sentenced to 10 years in prison. Among the charges brought against him was his order of 17 September 1942, when he ordered his commanders to cease helping survivors of torpedoed ships, after a U-boat was bombed by an American Liberator while rescuing the survivors of the troopship *Laconia*. He was sent to Spandau Prison in Berlin but was released in 1956 and thereafter lived in seclusion. He died on 24 December 1980, at the age of 89.

The Type IXC/40 *U-190*, commanded by Oberleutnant zur See Hans-Edwin Reith, approaching a mooring at St John's in Newfoundland after surrendering on 14 May 1945. Commissioned on 24 September 1942, this U-boat sank 2 Allied ships in 32 months of active service. One was the minesweeper HMCS *Esquimalt*, of 672 tons displacement, which was torpedoed on 16 April 1945 off Halifax, Nova Scotia, with the loss of forty-four men.

Bruce Robertson collection

On 30 December 1943 a formation of Typhoon IBs of 266 (Rhodesia) Squadron from Harrowbeer in Devon was on an offensive patrol off the north-west coast of France when this Junkers Ju52/3m g6e(MS) 'Mausi' of 1. Minensuchgruppe, fitted with a mine-detonating dural hoop, was spotted near the Ile de Croix. Two Typhoons, flown by Flying Officers W.V. Mollett and N.J. Lucas, were ordered to attack and sent the enemy machine crashing into the sea. There was no sign of survivors. The hydraulics of the Typhoon flown by Flying Officer N.J. Lucas were damaged by flying debris and he made a belly-landing back at Harrowbeer.

Author's collection

At almost midday on 6 January 1944 Sunderland III serial EK586 of 10 (RAAF) Squadron, flown by Flying Officer J.P. Roberts from Mount Batten in Devon, came across a U-boat on the surface about 400 miles west of St Nazaire. This was the *U-426*, commanded by Kapitänleutnant Christian Reich, which had left Brest 5 days before and was headed for the North Atlantic. It was on its second war cruise, having sunk the merchant vessel *Essex Lance* of 5,625 tons on its first cruise. Roberts attacked, with his front gunner opening fire and silencing the gunners in the conning tower, but the bomb trolley failed to run out. Six depth-charges were dropped on a second attack and the U-boat sank with all fifty-one hands.

*Wing Commander John C. Graham DFC**

The crew of the Type VIIC *U-960* being welcomed on 3 February 1944 by the Commander-in-Chief of the 3rd U-Flotilla at La Pallice, on arrival from a war cruise in the North Atlantic. The *U-960* had set out from Trondheim on 14 December 1944.

Fregattenkapitän a.D. Günther Heinrich

The American armed merchant vessel *Sumner I Kimball*, of 7,176 tons, was torpedoed on 16 January 1944 in the North Atlantic by the Type VIIC *U-960*. Men in the U-boat watched the ship's crew get into the lifeboats, put on their lights and set off. They were rescued by US destroyers.

Fregattenkapitän a.D. Günther Heinrich

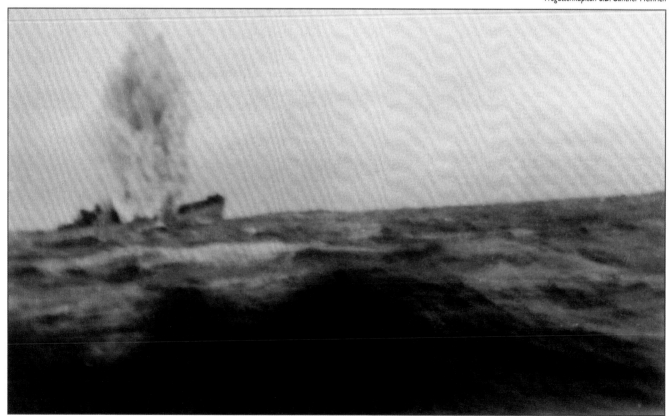

This Type VIIC, *U-625*, left Brest on 29 February 1944 for a war cruise under the command of Oberleutnant zur See Siegfried Straub. It was attacked 10 days later when west of Ireland by Sunderland III serial EK591 of 422 (RCAF) Squadron, flown from Castle Archdale in Northern Ireland by Flight Lieutenant S.W. Butler. The U-boat and the Sunderland exchanged fire and both were hit. Butler then dropped six depth-charges which straddled the target, as shown here. The U-boat submerged but resurfaced a few minutes later and signalled by lamp to the RAF crew, congratulating them on their bombing accuracy. It sank over an hour later, leaving some men in the water. None of the fifty-three men in the crew survived.

Author's collection

Oberleutnant zur See Helmut Rosenbaum,
commander of the Type VIIB *U-73*, working at his chart
table with First Watch Officer Horst Deckert and
crew member Karl Keller looking on. This U-boat was
sunk off the coast of Algeria on 16 December 1943,
when under the command of Oberleutnant zur See
Deckert, by the US destroyers *Woolsey* and *Trippe*. In
all, 16 of the crew were killed and 24 were rescued.

U-Boot-Archiv, Cuxhaven-Altenbruch

Catalina VIA serial JK694 of 210 Squadron, fitted with
a nacelle-type Leigh Light under the starboard wing
and Mark II Air to Surface-Vessel radar, photographed
in 1944 when the squadron was based at Sullom Voe
in the Shetlands.

Author's collection

The escort carrier HMS *Chaser*, of 10,700 tons displacement, on lease-lend from the USA, viewed from a Fairey Swordfish which had just taken off from the flight deck. The photograph was taken around the time when the M class destroyer HMS *Mahratta*, of 1,540 tons displacement, was sunk on 25 February 1944 by a torpedo fired from the Type VIIC *U-990* about 280 miles west of the North Cape of Norway.

Author's collection

Commander S.T.C. Harrison, commanding
HMS *Furious*, briefing aircrews of the Fleet Air Arm
with the aid of a relief map of Altenfjord in Norway,
prior to a major attack on 3 April 1944 against the
battleship *Tirpitz*. Barracuda bombers, escorted by
Seafire, Wildcat, Hellcat and Corsair fighters, were
detailed for the attack. The aircraft were on board the
fleet carriers HMS *Victorious* and HMS *Furious*, together
with the escort carriers HMS *Searcher*, HMS *Emperor*
and HMS *Pursuer*. These warships from the Home
Fleet were under the command of Vice-Admiral Sir
Henry R. Moore.

Author's collection

Barracuda bombers approaching Altenfjord for their attack against the *Tirpitz*. They set off on 3 April 1944 in two waves, each of the 21 Barracudas escorted by fighters, the first at 04.15 hours and the second at 05.25 hours. Some aircraft carried a single 1,600lb armour-piercing bomb, others carried three 500lb semi-armour-piercing bombs and others carried three 600lb anti-submarine bombs. The crews had been briefed to attack from various levels while the fighters raked enemy gun positions and the deck of the *Tirpitz*. One Barracuda in the first wave failed to start and another crashed in the sea after take-off.

Author's collection

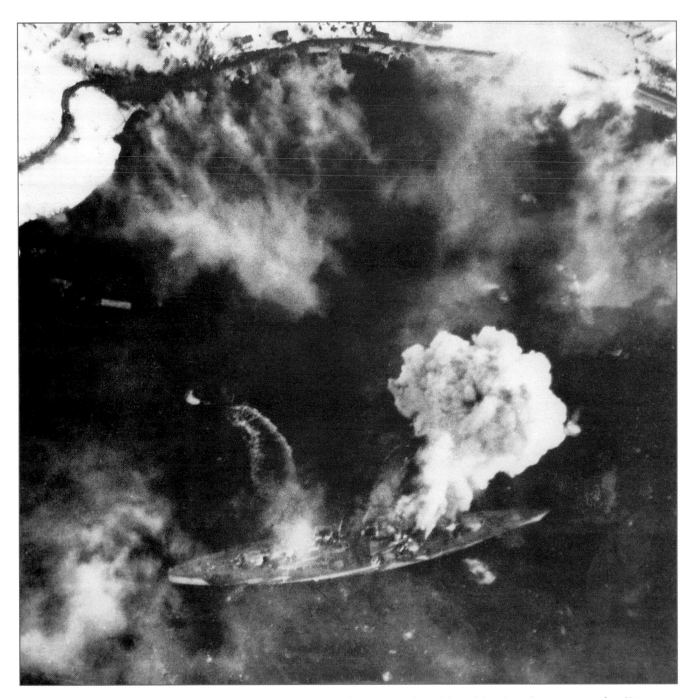

The first wave achieved complete surprise. No enemy fighters were encountered and defensive gunfire was not opened up until the attack began. It was all over in one minute. Several hits were seen but one bomber and one fighter did not return. A smokescreen began to shield the battleship but the second wave arrived about an hour later and achieved more hits. One Barracuda was shot down. It appears that the *Tirpitz* was hit by nine bombs and additionally damaged by near misses, but no bombs penetrated the armoured deck. Nevertheless she was out of commission for three months.

Author's collection

The Type VIIC *U-959*, commanded by Oberleutnant zur See Friedrich Weitz, outside Dora I bunker at Trondheim. It was sunk south-east of Jan Mayen Island in the late afternoon of 2 May 1944 by depth-charges dropped from a Swordfish of 842 Squadron, Fleet Air Arm, flown by Sub-Lieutenant L.G. Cooper from the escort carrier HMS *Fencer* on a Russian convoy. There were no survivors.

U-Boot-Archiv, Cuxhaven-Altenbruch

This Short Sunderland was forced down into the sea by engine trouble when on a transit flight, but made a safe touch-down apart from losing its port float. High Speed Launch HSL2725 came out to rescue the passengers and give the flying boat a tow. The photograph is dated 6 May 1944.

Author's collection

Rockets with 25lb solid-shot warheads being fitted in
February 1945 to the underwing rails of Mosquito IV
serial PZ438 of 143 Squadron at Banff. These rockets
were aimed at the sea immediately in front of an
enemy vessel, so that they curved slightly upwards on
impact and penetrated the hull below the waterline.

RAF Museum P100153

One of the Loch class frigates, of 1,435 tons displacement and capable of 19.5 knots, which served in the Royal Canadian Navy from 1944. These were considered the most effective 'U-boat killers' of the war. They were armed with a 4-inch gun, a variety of anti-aircraft weapons and two triple anti-submarine 'Squid' mortars. This example, photographed in May 1945, was fitted with a Type 277 10cm radar on the 'Starfish' mounting on the foremast and a Type S25B HF/DF at the masthead.

Roger Hayward collection

In the early afternoon of 8 July 1944 Sunderland III serial W4030 of 10 (RAAF) Squadron, flown by Flying Officer William B. Tilley from Mount Batten in Devon, picked up a U-boat on his radar when about 225 miles west of St Nazaire. This was the Type VIIC *U-243*, under the command of Kapitänleutnant Hans Märtens, which had left Bergen on 15 June and was headed for the English Channel to attack the western flank of the Allied invasion force. Tilley dropped six depth-charges which crippled the U-boat, while an exchange of fire took place between his gunners and those on the conning tower. The U-boat was then attacked by another Sunderland of 10 (RAAF) Squadron and a Liberator of the US VP-105 Squadron. It sank, but Tilley helped the survivors by dropping a dinghy and thirty-nine men were rescued by the destroyer HMCS *Restigouche*. These included the commander, but he subsequently died of his injuries.

*Wing Commander John C. Graham DFC**

The Curtiss SC-1 was a single-seat reconnaissance aircraft designed for the US Navy as a floatplane which would be easily converted to wheeled landing gear. Powered by a Wright R-1820-62 Cyclone 9 engine and armed with two 0.50-inch machine-guns, it could carry up to 650lb of bombs. The first were delivered to the US Navy in October 1944.

Bruce Robertson collection

The end of the Type IXC/40 *U-867*, commanded by Kapitänleutnant zur See Arved Mühlendahl, came on 19 September 1944 when it was attacked north-west of Bergen by a Liberator V of 224 Squadron, flown from Milltown in Morayshire by Flight Lieutenant H.J. Rayner. The Liberator dropped six depth-charges while under accurate fire from enemy gunners. This U-boat had already been seriously damaged the previous day during an attack by the Banff Strike Wing. This consisted of four Mosquito VIs of 248 Squadron which fired cannon or dropped depth-charges, two Mosquito XVIIIs (Tsetses) of 248 Squadron which fired 6-pounder guns, and two Mosquito VIs of 235 Squadron which provided fighter escort. The attack by the Liberator caused further damage and the commander was forced to scuttle his boat. In spite of the numerous dinghies with survivors, floating in a patch of oil, all sixty crew members perished in the freezing seas.

Bruce Robertson collection

Men in the conning tower of the Type VIIC *U-960* in the North Atlantic during bad weather in November 1943. The periscope in the foreground was later hit by a shell fired by a Tsetse.

Fregattenkapitän a.D. Günther Heinrich

Oberleutnant zur See Günther 'Heini' Heinrich, commander of the Type VIIC *U-960*, photographed in February 1944 after arriving at La Pallice from a war cruise.

Fregattenkapitän a.D. Günther Heinrich

The nose cone of the Tsetse of 248 Squadron flown on 27 March 1944 by Flying Officer A.H. 'Hilly' Hilliard, after being struck by a 37-mm shell fired by the Type VIIC *U-960*. The shell did not explode.

A.H. Hilliard

A.H. 'Hilly' Hilliard holding a dummy shell in 1989. It is similar in appearance to the live shells he fired at *U-960* from his Tsetse on 27 March 1944.

A.H. Hilliard

Two former enemies, 'Hilly' Hilliard (left) and 'Heini' Heinrich, pictured in Hamburg on 21 May 1989.

A.H. Hilliard

British prisoners repatriated from Germany arriving at Liverpool in the 'mercy ship' *Atlantis* of 15,135 tons, to the cheers of a welcoming crowd. These men had been seriously wounded and some were blinded. Wounded German prisoners were also repatriated to their homeland, via the Red Cross.

Author's collection

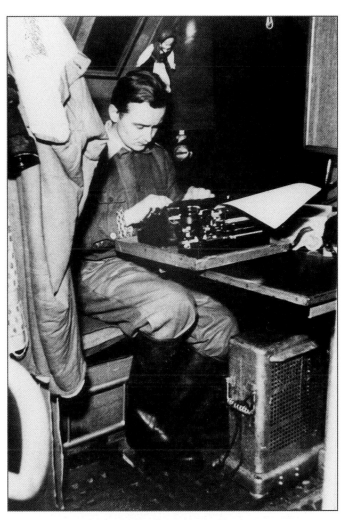

Oberleutnant zur See Wilhelm Gerlach, commander of the Type XIV supply boat *U-490*, working in his tiny 'cabin' with the comfort of a portable heater. His cabin was situated in the main corridor but could be cut off by a heavy curtain. His U-boat was depth-charged and sunk when north-west of the Azores on 12 June 1944 by the US destroyers *Frost*, *Huse* and *Inch*, part of a convoy which included the escort carrier HMS *Croatan*. Sixty men from the crew were rescued.

U-Boot-Archiv, Cuxhaven-Altenbruch

The rock of Gibraltar is well illustrated in this night photograph of a Douglas Dakota of the British Overseas Airways Corporation, silhouetted against searchlights while waiting for take-off in November 1944.

Author's collection

The heaviest loss of life along the Norwegian coast occurred on 27 November 1944 when Barracudas and Fireflies of the Fleet Air Arm from HMS *Implacable* attacked a German convoy off the Norwegian island of Rosöya. This convoy, from Finland headed to Mosjöen, consisted of the troopship *Rigel* with the merchant vessels *Korsnes* and *Spree*, escorted by the flak ships V6308 *Saturn* and NT04 *Salier*. The *Rigel* of 3,828 tons was set on fire and grounded, as seen here. The *Korsnes*, *Saturn* and *Salier* were badly hit and also grounded. But the *Rigel* was carrying 2,248 Russian and Serbian prisoners, 95 German deserters and 8 Norwegian prisoners, as well as German guards and the ship's crew. Only 250 of these men survived.

Author's collection

The flash of light from a 6-pounder shell fired by a Tsetse of 248 Squadron during an attack by the Banff Strike Wing on vessels in Eidfjord on 12 December 1944. It hit the German merchant vessel *Wartheland* of 3,768 tons, which sank.

Author's collection

This merchant vessel, the German *Ferndale* of 5,684 tons, was attacked on 16 December 1944 by 22 Mosquitos of the Banff Strike Wing while in the narrow fjord of Krahellesund in Norway.
She was badly hit and her destruction was completed by 6 more Mosquitos which arrived an hour later. A Mosquito from the first formation was forced to ditch and another from the second attack
was also shot down.

Author's collection

The German destroyer Z-37, of 2,603 tons displacement and armed with five 15-cm guns, was one of the warships which operated in the Bay of Biscay after the fall of France. She was scuttled by the Germans at Bordeaux on 25 August 1944, to prevent her falling into the hands of the Allies.

Author's collection

A Consolidated Liberator of Coastal Command flying over the mountains of Iceland en route to a 16-hour flight on convoy escort in the North Atlantic.

Author's collection

The last attack made by the Fleet Air Arm in the European theatre took place on 4 May 1945 when 16 Avengers and 28 Wildcats took off from the aircraft carriers HMS *Queen*, HMS *Searcher* and HMS *Trumpeter* to attack enemy vessels at Kilbotn, near Harstad in Norway. They sank the submarine depot ship *Black Watch* of 5,039 tons, the Type VIIC U-boat *U-711* and the freighter *Senja* of 850 tons. They also damaged the torpedo supply ship *Admiral Carl Hering* of 1,436 tons. Forty men were killed in *U-711* but the commander, Kapitänleutnant Hans-Günther Lange, and eleven seamen survived. The vessel in the left foreground is the anti-aircraft ship *Thetis* of 3,858 tons.

Author's collection

After the attack of 9 April 1945 in which *U-804* and *U-1065* were sunk by the Banff Strike Wing, Flying Officer A.J. Randell of 235 Squadron began to escort home a damaged Mosquito, but when the pilot said he could reach Banff on his own, Randell returned to the scene of the battle. Here he found another U-boat, the Type IXC/40 *U-843*, commanded by Kapitänleutnant Oskar Herwartz. This ocean-going U-boat had made three war cruises, one to the Azores and two blockade runs to the Far East. It was making for Kiel from Bergen. Randell fired rockets and cannon shells from his Mosquito, scoring numerous direct hits. *U-843* sank with all forty-four hands.

Wing Commander John C. Graham DFC*

In the morning of 2 May 1945 33 Mosquitos of the Banff Strike Wing with an escort of Mustangs went hunting U-boats in the Kattegat. They came across two boats, including the Type XXIII *U-2559* commanded by Oberleutnant zur See G. Bischoff, and attacked with rockets, cannon fire and Molins guns. The U-boats were en route from Kiel to Horten in Norway. *U-2559* was sunk while the other U-boat was damaged.

Author's collection

The Type IXC/40 *U-534*, commanded by Kapitänleutnant Herbert Nollau, was one of the last U-boats to be sunk in the war. It was one of three U-boats discovered sailing together on the surface in the Kattegat on 5 May 1945 by Liberator III serial KH347 of 86 Squadron, flown from Tain in Ross & Cromarty by Warrant Officer J.D. Nicol. Another Liberator, of 547 Squadron, flown from Leuchars in Fife by Flight Lieutenant G.W. Hill, was seen to make two attacks on the three U-boats, but was shot down by flak. Nicol then dropped six depth-charges on the U-boat in the rear. This sank stern first, leaving survivors in the water. Only three men of *U-534* were killed, forty-nine being picked up by rescue craft from Denmark. One man from the crashed Liberator was also picked up.

Bruce Robertson collection

A Type XXI electro-boat at Kiel towards the end of the war. There was deep water in the bay and U-boats were laid on the sea bottom when there was any danger of air attack.

U-Boot-Archiv, Cuxhaven-Altenbruch

A Type IX U-boat, flying the black flag of surrender, photographed about 250 miles west of
Land's End in the early afternoon of 11 May 1945 by Sunderland K of 461 (RAAF) Squadron,
flown from Pembroke Dock by Flight Lieutenant R.R. Alexander.

Bruce Robertson collection

Two Type XXIII electro-boats at Lisahilly in Northern Ireland, after surrendering at the end
of the war. This was one of two places in Britain where surrendered U-boats were held after
examination. These were the smaller type of electro-boats, designed for operations in coastal
waters.

Jak P. Mallmann Showell collection

The Type VIIC *U-995* at Laboe near Kiel, where it is open to the public as a technical museum. It has a 37-mm gun aft of the conning tower and is also armed with two sets of twin 20-mm cannon. This boat was commissioned on 16 September 1943 and decommissioned on 8 May 1945. It completed eight war cruises in the Arctic, during which it sank 4 vessels and damaged another. Over 30,000 men who served in the front line of the U-boat arm lost their lives.

Fregattenkapitän a.D. Günther Heinrich

A close-up of the Type VIIC *U-995* at Laboe near Kiel, with the 37-mm gun on the left and twin 20-mm cannon on the right.

Jak P. Mallmann Showell collection

The Naval Memorial at Laboe near Kiel, photographed in 1999.

Jak. P. Mallmann Showell collection

Two memorials at the U-Boot-Archiv in Cuxhaven-Altenbruch.

Jak P. Mallmann Showell collection

This bronze figure of an 'Unknown Airman' in flying kit was sculpted by Pam Taylor. It was unveiled on 3 September 1989 as the main feature of the International Air Monument at Plymouth Hoe. Panels on the column pay tribute to RAF and USAAF leaders, in addition to commemorating those lost during the Second World War. These include 107,000 members of the RAF, 84,000 of the US Air Services, and 42,000 of the Soviet Air Force. Within the RAF losses were 58,378 in Bomber Command, 13,225 in Coastal Command, 7,436 in Fighter Command, 13,225 in the Middle East and 6,182 in South-East Asia.

Squadron Leader Ian Coleman RAF

A memorial to those who died serving in the Fleet Air Arm stands in Victoria Embankment Gardens in London, in front of the Ministry of Defence main building and facing south over the Thames.

Author's collection

Figures on the monument to the Merchant Navy in Trinity Gardens, near the Tower of London. Bronze plaques on the walls of the gardens record the names of about 24,000 men of the Merchant Navy and the Fishing Fleets who were killed in the Second World War and have 'no grave but the sea', under the names of their ships. The total losses in the Merchant Navy were 43,248 men.

Author's collection

These stone figures form part of the memorial to the Royal Navy at Plymouth Hoe. The original memorial was unveiled to commemorate the names of 7,256 men and women who died in the First World War, and then much enlarged to include the names of 15,926 more who lost their lives in the Second World War. The memorial is one of a series erected at each major base port of the Royal Navy. The total losses of the Royal Navy in the Second World War are listed as 73,642.

Squadron Leader Ian Coleman RAF

BIBLIOGRAPHY

Ashworth, Chris. *RAF Coastal Command 1936–1969*. Sparkford: Patrick Stephens, 1992.

Barnett, Correlli. *Engage the Enemy More Closely*. London: Penguin, 1991.

Brown, David. *Warship Losses of World War Two*. London: Arms & Armour Press, 1990.

Cremer, Peter. *U333*. London: The Bodley Head, 1984.

Enever, Ted. *Britain's Best Kept Secret*. Stroud: Sutton, 1999.

Franks, Norman. *Search, Find and Kill*. London: Grub Street, 1995.

Goss, Chris. *Bloody Biscay*. Manchester: Crécy, 1997.

Hinsley, F.H. et al. *British Intelligence in the Second World War* (6 vols). HMSO, 1979–1990.

Kaplan, Philip & Currie, Jack. *Convoy*. London: Arum Press, 1998.

Macintyre, Donald. *The Battle of the Atlantic*. London: Batsford, 1961.

Niestlé, Axel. *German U-boat Losses during World War II*. London: Greenhill, 1998.

Philpott, Bryan. *German Maritime Aircraft*. Cambridge: Patrick Stephens, 1981.

Price, Alfred. *Aircraft versus Submarine*. London: William Kimber, 1979.

Public Record Office:

AIR 41/73 *The RAF in Maritime War, Vol. 2*, September 1939–June 1941.

AIR 41/47 *The RAF in Maritime War, Vol. 3*, July 1941–February 1943.

AIR 41/48 *The RAF in Maritime War, Vol. 4*, February 1943–May 1944.

AIR 41/74 *The RAF in Maritime War, Vol. 5*, June 1944–May 1945.

Richards, Denis & Saunders, Hilary St G. *Royal Air Force 1939–45* (3 vols). HMSO, 1953–1954.

Roskill, S.W. *The War at Sea* (3 vols). HMSO, 1954–1961.

Sharp, Peter. *U-boat Fact File*. Leicester: Midland, 1998.

Showell, Jak P. Mallmann. *Enigma U-boats*. Shepperton: Ian Allan, 2000.

——. *U-boats under the Swastika*. Shepperton: Ian Allan, 1987.

Spooner, Tony. *Coastal Ace*. London: William Kimber, 1986.

Sturtivant, Ray. *British Naval Aviation*. London: Arms & Armour Press, 1990.

Tarrant, V.E. *The Last Year of the Kriegsmarine*. London: Arms & Armour Press, 1994.

Terraine, John. *Business in Great Waters*. Ware: Wordsworth, 1999.

Tusa, Ann & Tusa, John. *The Nuremberg Trial*. London: BBC Books, 1995.

Von Müllenheim-Rechburg. *Battleship Bismarck*. London: The Bodley Head, 1981.

Welchman, Gordon. *The Hut Six Story*. Cleobury Mortimer: Baldwin, 1998.

Books by the same author

Woe to the Unwary

Torpedo Airmen

The Strike Wings

Target: Hitler's Oil (with Ronald C. Cooke)

Arctic Airmen (with Ernest Schofield)

Failed to Return

An Illustrated History of the RAF

RAF Records in the PRO (with Simon Fowler, Peter Elliott and Christina Goulter)

The Armed Rovers

Eyes of the RAF

The RAF in Camera, 1903–1939

The RAF in Camera, 1939–1945

The RAF in Camera, 1945–1995

RAF Coastal Command in Action, 1939–1995

RAF: An Illustrated History from 1918

Britain's Rebel Air Force (with Dudley Cowderoy and Andrew Thomas)

The Flight of Rudolf Hess (with Georges van Acker)

RAF in Action, 1939–1945

The Battle of Britain

INDEX